Roehenstart

A LATE STUART PRETENDER

. . . pretenders, to anything big enough,
have always been, for me,
an attractive class.

—Henry James, *A Passionate Pilgrim.*

ambition should be made of sterner stuff.

—Shakespeare.

Roehenstart

A Late Stuart Pretender

Being
An Account of the Life of
Charles Edward August Maximilien Stuart
Baron Korff Count Roehenstart

By GEORGE SHERBURN

THE UNIVERSITY OF CHICAGO PRESS

Library of Congress Catalog Number: 60–8402

The University of Chicago Press, Chicago 37
Oliver and Boyd, Edinburgh
The University of Toronto Press, Toronto 5, Canada

Composed and printed in Great Britain

Preface

This volume presents a pioneer sketch of the life of a gentleman who at times called himself "the last of the Stuarts," and pretty certainly was the grandson of Prince Charles Edward, the Young Pretender to the British throne. It is largely based on the man's personal papers, purchased by the author on April 8, 1935, in a sale at Sotheby's. They are a highly miscellaneous lot of loose papers in at least a half-dozen languages, notably English, French, Italian, German, and Russian—with bits of modern Greek, Gaelic, and Spanish thrown in. As here printed, documents written in a language other than English have been translated. One may doubt if Roehenstart had (as most of us have) a native language; his faulty idioms (which make translation risky) may at times, however, be set down merely to hasty writing.

Roehenstart must have known that he was not a legitimate son, and to conceal his somewhat scandalous paternity, he used his imagination in creating for himself a respectable Swedish father, whom he knew to be quite fictitious. His title, Count Roehenstart, suggests a Continental pronunciation of Rohan-Stuart. Evidently one fiction led to another, and not all of his merely imaginative statements can be surely detected as such. Further complication arises from the diversity of his intellectual interests and his personal connections in several countries. These, partly revealed or merely hinted, increase the obscurity inherent in a fragmentary archive; but the unified skeleton of a varied picaresque career emerges clearly.

Apart from the papers now in the possession of the author, and presently to go to the Bodleian Library, the chief documents of use in the work are the letters of Charlotte Stuart to her mother, Clementine Walkinshaw, now already in the Bodleian (North MSS. d. 27, 28). In 1935 the author first read these letters, and was later pleased to find that when, at his suggestion, the learned Henrietta Tayler read them again, she agreed that they showed definitely that before Charlotte Stuart went to Florence to live with her father, she had given birth to three children, still living in 1789. Other manuscripts in the British Museum, the Archives Nationales (Paris), and the Houghton Library at Harvard, have proved useful.

Most, but not all, of the facts here presented, are published for the first time. Shortly after 1935 the author sent to the late Henrietta Tayler information drawn from the papers, with permission to publish. She used details freely in her book *Prince Charlie's Daughter* (1950). In a few cases the information was too hastily sent, and some details are here corrected.

In the early stages of the work the author had valuable aid from Miss Tayler and from A. Francis Steuart, both now unfortunately deceased. More recently he has been aided by Rev. J. Edgar Bruns, S.T.D., and in much indispensable information and advice by C. L. Berry.

Contents

I.	*Parentage*	1
II.	*Early Years*	15
III.	*Russia: 1807–11*	22
IV.	*America: 1812–14*	30
V.	*The Tin Box*	39
VI.	*The Memorial (1816)*	51
VII.	*Reactions*	65
VIII.	*Early Aftermath*	75
IX.	*Travels*	87
X.	*Last Journeyings*	109
XI.	*A Note on Finances*	118
XII.	*The Anatomy of Pretending*	124
APPENDIXES		
I.	*"The Case of X against Y"*	131
II.	*Summaries of Letters to Mrs. Stuart*	134
III.	*The Battle of Saalfeld (1806)*	137
INDEX		145

CHAPTER ONE

Parentage

Roehenstart's father and mother, untrained and irregular in their lives as they were, had more distinguished careers than the son was to have. His mother was Charlotte Stuart, legitimated daughter of Prince Charles Edward, who, if things had gone according to his heart's desire, would have been King Charles III of England. She was born at Liége in 1753 and died at Bologna on November 15, 1789. Her mother was Clementine Walkinshaw, whom Prince Charles had met in the Highlands during his furtive wanderings of 1745 after the failure of the invasion of that year. When safely back on the Continent the Prince asked Clementine to join him there, and she very promptly did. They met at Ghent, and thereafter lived together, flitting from one town to another as Count and Countess Johnson. Any marriage of these two would have been irregular without the approval of the Prince's father, the "Old Pretender," and it is practically certain that there never was any marriage. The first seven years of Charlotte Stuart's life must have been strange for the child—passed in Liége, Bâle, Boulogne, and other towns. In 1760 Clementine, weary of the vagrant and violent life with Prince Charles, appealed to the Prince's father for protection and for aid in the education of the small daughter. The result was a midnight flight from Boulogne and from Prince Charles that took the mother and daughter to Paris. For years thereafter the two were housed in various convents, either at Meaux or in Paris. At this time or earlier the Emperor Francis II had given the mother the title of Countess of Albestroff (sometimes wrongly printed as Albertroff). She had a pension from James III, who, however, did not see her. Prince Charles meanwhile was furious at her desertion of him and apparently never saw her again.

Upon the death of James III in 1766, the Countess of Albestroff appealed to the brother of Prince Charles, Henry, Cardinal-Duke of York, to continue the pension. He was more difficult than his father had been, and ultimately, through threats and promises about the pension, persuaded the Countess to sign a statement that she had never been married to the Prince. The document was useful in 1772 in aiding the marriage arranged between Prince Charles and the twenty-year-old Princess Louise of Stolberg. The marriage was in every way a failure. No heir resulted. Charles seemed unfortunately averse to any society that did not recognize his royal pretensions; and Louise was charming, vivacious, and amorous. In less than a decade she left her husband for the poet Alfieri, and in 1784 a formal separation was arranged. The Cardinal-Duke continued to pay her a pension as dowry, and later the British government, secure in her assertion that she had never had a child, paid her annually the sum of £1,600. The generous financial arrangements made for "Queen" Louise doubtless stimulated Roehenstart to imagine that he also might have something done for him.

The marriage of Prince Charles was naturally a stunning blow to the Countess of Albestroff and her daughter. It seemed to close the door on them, and even to threaten the loss of their pension. It is not true, as has been said, that they were in Rome when Prince Charles's bride arrived there. She arrived in the spring of 1772 (the marriage was celebrated on Good Friday!) and Clementine and Charlotte did not come to Rome until the summer of 1773. Why they came is a mystery. They had tried to prepare the way by sending from Meaux the formal felicitations that were appropriate at New Year's. Prince Charles Edward was born on December 31, a fact that gave the felicitations double validity. Mother and daughter sent their greetings both to Prince Charles and to the Cardinal-Duke. The tone of Charlotte's note to her father is affectionate and pleading. She hopes he will recognize her continuing affection: "It is in this hope that I dare to renew for you the urgent petitions already made by me and that I dare hope you will at last wish to grant me a good that I value above all others and without which these others would be nothing—the honour of being known to belong to you. In the hope of meriting your acknowledgment and affection I shall continue every effort to make myself worthy of that favour."

Prince Charles must have had some kindly feeling for the child who had been taken from him a dozen years before, but if he answered her plea (which is most doubtful) the answer has not been found. In 1772 the Prince married Louise von Stolberg, and in 1773 Clementine and Charlotte arrived in Rome. Their journey was so little lacking in discretion that it makes one wonder. Possibly Charlotte, thinking that pleasant early attachments might soften a father's heart, imagined that even the briefest meeting might suffice to win the end desired. That was at least the attitude of her son later with regard to an audience with the Prince Regent of England in 1816.

Apparently no audience was granted, and the two ladies were ordered to leave Rome at once. Charlotte in a letter to the secretary of the Cardinal-Duke (June 23, 1773) called the orders severe but professed "entire obedience." She begged that she and her mother might remove from Meaux to Paris, and that change was evidently allowed. Charlotte, now twenty years old, was perhaps hopeful that if only her father would grant a dowry, she might as the daughter of an exiled prince find a husband. Lacking a dowry, hope grew faint. No longer a girl, Charlotte probably before 1780 became secretly the mistress of her cousin, Prince Ferdinand de Rohan-Guéméné, whom she seems to have adored intermittently for the rest of her life. He was fifteen years her senior. Love apart, this affair was a tragic mistake (there were three children from it); for shortly, in 1780, the wife of Prince Charles fled from the Palazzo San Clemente and from her husband. Her liaison with Alfieri was by 1783 so unconcealed that a formal separation from Prince Charles was presently arranged.

The Prince, now left lonely, in 1783 legitimated his daughter and invited her to come and live with him in Florence. She was to have the rank of royal highness and the title of Duchess of Albany. Prince Charles, in circles where his kingship was not recognized, used the Scottish title of Count of Albany. His wife was known as Countess of Albany, and for purposes of precedence (?) his daughter was to be Duchess of Albany. The Countess of Albestroff may have doubted if even the title of duchess would repay for a life with the princely temper which she knew too well; but for her daughter there could be no hesitation. It meant an end to their equivocal position and to their life of penury. Prince Ferdinand was neither very wealthy nor responsibly generous. As the recognized daughter of a "king" there might be a future. Even marriage was a possibility, though Charlotte probably did not desire that; more prosperous days were a certainty. A king must have money: she and her mother could pay their debts and live happily ever afterward. Prince Charles was in his sixties and ailing, and, so Charlotte believed, his house must be full of gold and diamonds.

One can only set her down as a poor deluded young woman—but courageous.

In her letters from Italy to her mother in Paris we get a vivid picture of Charlotte's last years. She must frequently hide a meaning or write in a sort of cipher language; for letters might be opened and read by enemies. Prince Ferdinand, for example, is never mentioned by name. He is always called *mon amis* or *mon digne amis*. Prince Ferdinand had in 1781 become the archbishop-duke of Cambrai, and *mon amis* is at times called "the archbishop" and spoken of as being in Cambrai. When his brother the "necklace" Cardinal gets into trouble and is banished, the Cardinal is spoken of as "the brother of mon amis." The correspondence (preserved in the Bodleian Library) includes one letter from Prince Ferdinand to the Countess of Albestroff, and the handwriting and monogram signature are certainly identical with letters preserved in the British Museum and in the Archives Nationales that are Prince Ferdinand's.

In writing to her mother Charlotte never mentions her children as such. She uses for "nursery" the common metaphor of a garden: *mon petit jardin* is a frequent, affectionate topic, and she speaks once of a possible child by a rival, which, if placed in her garden would "crowd my plants." There were three of her "friends" as she commonly calls the children. The oldest apparently was Aglae—old enough in 1789 to have masters and wish to have a watch. Another was possibly called Zemire; at least once in speaking of these "friends" the Duchess continues with, "and how is Zemire?" In some (unauthenticated) traditions this child is named Marie. The third child is the subject of this book, and he is never mentioned by name. That the children numbered three is certain from the mother's usual conclusion that sends three kisses to them.

After an unexplained delay of eighteen months from the time when she was invited to come and live with her father, Charlotte finally reached Florence, and letters began to come back to her mother. She was speedily aware of difficulties to be faced. Her father was indeed *regardeur* when it came to money, and to her mother Charlotte could be frank in avowing money as her chief object. She was paying her debts as fast as possible: she did not wish her father to be much aware of her creditors. She wishes she could send the wealth of Peru to her mother, but debts come first. Six months after her arrival in Florence she could still dream of "collecting millions," though meanwhile happy on an allowance. After they removed to Rome she got some jewels, and was eager to know how much her ruby and her two sets of diamonds might bring in cash.

Her father's imperious rages were trying, and so were the social excitements in Florence. To the daughter Prince Charles did not seem the gloomy unsocial personage that the wife had found him. Charlotte reports wearily (her health was not good), that her father loved carnival "as if he were still sixteen." The new life was far more stirring than anything known in the Rue St. Jacques in Paris. In January she pictures Prince Charles as normally active: "My father goes on calmly. He goes walking in spite of wind or storm. His head bows from day to day. I am glad to have been able to get him to do for us what we desire." In April, however, he suffers from gout: "For eight days my father has been in continual rages: he shouts, he storms without rhyme or reason. Wine is not the cause: he drinks almost none; but surely the humour in his leg mounts to his brain." When the "gout" got into the brain, as they thought in the eighteenth century, it was fatal.

To secure the financial settlement desired, Charlotte presently realized that the co-operation of the Cardinal-Duke was essential. The Cardinal, on his side, desired a reconciliation with his brother, and Charlotte speedily was at work to bring it about. She was, perhaps, a born conciliator—though she almost certainly exaggerates her success as such. She had in Florence improved the management of her father's household; at least her early verdict had been, "We live like animals." She had the patience necessary for quiet diplomacy. "Que de patience!" she exclaims more than once. In a slightly higher mood she writes, "It's slow. Ah well, take courage. All will be for the best, I hope." And in her firmest mood she writes, "Tot ou tard je viendrez à bout." (Her French is frequently faulty.)

She first reconciled her father to the memory of Clementine. Early in 1785 he sends, so his daughter writes, compliments to his former mistress, now so long in disgrace. He talked of her, Charlotte says, at times tenderly, and at the beginning of the year 1787, he signed a dictated letter to her, "Votre bon ami Charles R." This letter, written by a secretary, Roehenstart got among his papers; but the reply from Clementine, which the daughter says delighted the "king," he did not get. Since the attitude of Prince Charles to his former mistress has been questioned, his letter to her is here translated:

Rome 3 January 1787

Madame the Countess, although I have charged my dear daughter the Duchess of Albany to tell you how much I was moved by your letter of the

18th of the past month, I cannot refrain from indicating also my sincere gratitude. The prayers that you address to heaven, the wishes that you make for my happiness and felicity I believe most sincere, and it seems that they may be realized since I enjoy perfect health, and I hope in return that you may always be in the same state. My dear daughter the Duchess of Albany is also at this moment in the best of health. The sweetness of her nature, her good qualities, and her amiable companionship diminish greatly the pains and inconveniences that are indispensably joined to my aged condition. Rest assured that I love her, and that I shall love her with all my heart all my life, and that I am and shall be Your good friend CHARLES R.

Doubtless Charlotte had brought about this possibly slight friendliness. She was also a helper when it came to reconciling the two royal brothers. At first the Cardinal had been averse to the recognition of his brother's daughter, but he wished a reconciliation with his brother, and the role of Charlotte in the matter is best known from a "Memoria"[1] written in Italian and sent to the Pope (Pius VI). It is undated, but was evidently written in 1785 before the "Royal Brother" and his new-found daughter left Florence for Rome. The Cardinal wrote (formally in the third person):

. . . when the Royal Brother sometime since legitimated his natural daughter, the Cardinal Duke found it a necessary duty to take certain indispensable steps out of annoyance concerning not merely the manner but some circumstances of this legitimation too disagreeable to him, and in truth contrary to all ordinary protocol, and more offensive still to his entire family and house. However, the fine nature of the young Lady legitimated impelled her to take up the matter with the Cardinal Duke and with such obliging importunity to begin a sort of correspondence in which with unusual justice the lady believed she should review every detail, writing him for this purpose a most obliging letter in which, giving him to understand that he need have nothing against her, she went on to clarify with all ingenuousness the just reasons for grief against the Royal Brother, but always in such phrases as, while remaining most diplomatic in her reasonings, she showed herself so contented that there followed a continued secret correspondence between them with such mutual satisfaction that the Cardinal Duke has had to conceive a true esteem for the young Lady and to admire her just manner of thinking and writing.

And now it appears that this Lady concealed this correspondence from the Royal Brother in order to serve him better, as she says. But the fact is that, in consequence of the wishes of the Cardinal Duke to remove through her aid the Royal Brother's very unjust prejudices against the Cardinal, the young Lady (whom one sees agreed to the last sign) has acted and managed so that she has

[1] The MS of this "Memoria" is now in the Harvard Library.

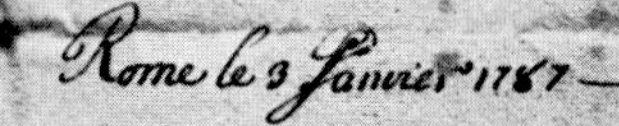

Rome le 3 Janvier 1787

Madame la Comtesse quoique j'aye chargé ma chere
Fille La Duchesse d'Albanie de vous exprimer combien
j'ai été sensible a votre lettre du 18 du mois passé, je ne
puis pas cependant m'empecher de vous marquer aussi ma
sincere reconnoissance. Les voeux que vous addressees
au Ciel, et les souhaites que vous faites pour mon
bonheur, et ma felicité je les crois les plus sinceres, et
il paroit que ils soyent exaussé, car je jouis d'une
parfaite santé, et je souhaite aussi que vous
soyez dans le meme etat a jamais. Ma Chere
fille la Duchesse d'Albanie jouit aussi de la meilleure
santé dans ce moment, la douceur de son naturel,
ses qualitees, et son aimable compagnie diminuent
de beaucoup les peines, et les incomoditees qui sont
indispensablement jointes a mon etat de Vieillesse.
Soyez assuree que je l'aime, et que je l'aimerai de
tout mon coeur toute ma vie, et que je suis, et
serai Votre bon Ami Charles R.

"Charles III" (Bonnie Prince Charlie) to His Estranged Mistress the Comtesse d'Albestroff

led him to write, as first, to the Cardinal Duke a most obliging letter from which one can foresee a true and lasting reconciliation.

After the removal to Rome the Cardinal frequently dined with Charlotte and presumably with Prince Charles in the Piazza SS. Apostoli. The young lady may have exaggerated her power over the Cardinal, but she constantly assured her mother that the Cardinal was madly devoted to her. According to her account the final step in reconciliation came late in October when "In the evening my father dined with him [the Cardinal] at Frascati. Our visit went off with much tenderness on one part or the other. On getting out of the carriages we were greeted with superb music. It was 15 years that my father had not set foot in his brother's house. . . ." The reconciliation was indeed a triumph; for by now Charlotte saw that the Cardinal was, so to speak, the treasurer of the household. His large income was the chief resource of the family at this time.

Charlotte was hardly more religious than her father, and she found in Rome that Lenten observances expected of royal personages were a considerable bore. Courage, or some other quality, dictated her decorous conduct, and the result was the sort of success that she well knew how to appreciate. Her final reconciliation was to be with the Holy Father himself. At considerable expense to his treasury Pius VI had had the Stuart palace at Albano redecorated and newly furnished, and in July, 1786, Charles and his daughter removed thither for the rest of the summer. Barring deaths and French revolutions one might have expected further long-term results from Charlotte's powers.

Meanwhile she was also a success in Roman society. A person who saw her there in the winter of 1786 describes her as follows:

> She was a tall, robust woman, of very dark complexion and coarse-grained skin, with more of masculine boldness than feminine modesty or elegance; but easy and unassuming in her manners, and amply possessed of that volubility of tongue, and that spirit of coquetry, for which the women of the country where she was educated have at all times been particularly distinguished.[1]

This not too flattering description does grant the lady an element of charm.

One must admit that her conduct owed its success to native good sense rather than to an extensive or thorough education. It is probable that before coming to Rome she was not much habituated to courtly circles. French was the only language she knew, and it she wrote very

[1] *Gentleman's Magazine*, 1797, p. 1000.

incorrectly. She probably had few accomplishments such as were desirable for young ladies; but her father loved music, and she worked at the harp and the pianoforte, and asked her mother to send music—"but nothing difficult." She worked hard to please and with considerable success. She was evidently one of the sights in Rome that English tourists flocked to see.

Not slowly she became aware of the difference between the life of a court, the life, so to speak, of a king's daughter and the dull routine of a convent—even though that routine were diminished by a concealed liaison. Perhaps to arouse jealousy in her *amis* she reported to her mother before leaving Florence that she had recently refused a brilliant *parti*: she still loved *mon amis* she declared. In Rome it became increasingly apparent that she could marry if she desired. There was talk of a possible match with the Pope's nephew or with the Irish Duke of Leinster, and she had a brief wistful thought of the fifth Duke of "Betford."

Reports of these and other projected matches, as given to her mother, aroused jealousy in Prince Ferdinand. When Prince Charles died (January 31, 1788) her Paris friends naturally expected a speedy return to France. But the settling of her father's estate, if nothing else, required her presence in Italy. As yet she had little to take back to France, and she did not relish the resumption of a state of poverty.

Prince Ferdinand was annoyed: she ought to return and begin to think of her "obligations." "I have replied to him," she magnificently writes to her mother, "that I know the whole extent of them, and that I will gladly in that matter walk in his footsteps." But presently Ferdinand was attempting political advancement: he wished to be prince-coadjutor of Liége, from which principality the Prussians had recently driven the Austrians. In Italy Charlotte might be useful to him. She had influence, and Ferdinand asked her to use it with powerful Prussian friends and with the Pope. For many reasons she was unable to help him much in his ambitions, though she thought she did get him a recommendation to the King of Prussia.

Time and separation had weakened the strong tie that had bound these two together. Each in fact doubted the other's loyalty; each was suspicious of the other. Lack of money was what irked Charlotte most. She had a small something, but not enough. She was, however, willing to be generous. Writing in January, 1785, she tells her mother, "What I give you will serve for your comfort and for the upkeep of my garden. My worthy friend has so fair a soul that I don't doubt that he will attend to everything, but for myself I wish to have my little part, for otherwise I should be jealous." In this early period of absence she remarks that she hopes *mon amis* will be content with his infant and will love and cherish it tenderly. In March, 1785, she writes obscurely, "I think that he who is in the country will soon come back to to the city. It's time in my opinion. I count on you entirely to watch over his health and see that he lacks nothing." These remarks are assumed to refer to the infant Roehenstart, though the reference is far from certain.

In the spring of 1788 there came a possible crisis that concerned the *petit jardin.* The house was leased from the Abbé de Villette for 1,800 livres. It was conveniently located "près les Dames de la Visitation, Rue St. Jacques." The Countess of Albestroff was authorized by her daughter to negotiate the new lease—at the old rental—for three years. The Duchess wrote in part: "I renew the lease for only three years, because I hope very much that before then we shall be reunited, and then the prolongation would be embarrassing. . . . Mon amis has notified me that he paid the rent. I replied that I hoped he would pay it again, because I regard him as *un bon papa.* I don't know how pleasing that proposition may be."

At this time Prince Ferdinand imagined that Charlotte had come into a kingly inheritance and was rich. In May, 1788, she wrote to him with sarcasm in reply to a request that she assume the entire expense of maintaining *nos amies.* So he seems to have continued, grumblingly, to pay the rent. At that moment civilization exploded with the fall of the Bastille, and Charlotte wrote, "Notre ami must think up a refuge for nos amies." Her mother seems to have thought the Faubourg St. Jacques a quiet spot, but Charlotte had no faith in Parisian tranquillity and urged her mother to take the children away from Paris. Clementine, however, was a native Scot, and with a three-year lease she seemed to have a roof over her head. Earlier in the summer she had been chaperoning about Paris the daughters of the London banker, Thomas Coutts, who was her remote relative—the only relative who in her last years of need befriended the Countess. Through her the Coutts daughters will later be a brief part of Roehenstart's story.

Charlotte's worry over her three small "friends" was intensified by her own ill health. It had been bad ever since she came to Italy, and even before. In June, 1786, she had written to her mother, "I have a swelling on my side which pains me when I breathe"; and in October she spoke of the tumor (?) as having been apparent "18 months ago." In view of her many activities her courage in concealing pain was remarkable. After the death of her father she was somewhat freer from duties, and in September, 1789, on advice of her doctors, she made a visit to watering places and seaside towns. October she was to spend in Bologna as guest of the Princess Lambertini. She seems in her letters no more worried about her health than usual. Her worries concerned her father's estate, and the painful fact that the Abbé Waters, her chosen executor, had searched the Palazzo San Clemente in Florence and found only a few jewels—no money. The long-sought provision for her family seemed slipping away.

Her letters during her travels at times admit that she feels much pain, but in general they are courageous, and in her very last letter preserved for us (October 10, 1789) she tries again to be reassuring: "Don't worry. I am well; I love you, and will as soon as possible send you news." When writing she must have known that surgery was both inevitable and very dangerous. The account given of her last days and her burial by the priest of the Church of the Holy Trinity in Bologna tells of her operation in four words: *incisionem forti animo sustinuit.* A brave mind, however, is no cure for gangrene, and on November 15 "ad primam noctis horam, presentibus Eminentissimis, adsistente huius Ecclesiae Parocho post dies triginta novem, placide Virgo regia obdormuit in Domino." The funeral was two days later. She had made the Cardinal her heir: she could hardly do otherwise unless she wished to publish her shame. Her presumable hopes that the Cardinal would do something for her family in Paris were vain, and it is perhaps not surprising that they explained the (to them) sudden and surprising death by suspicions of foul play.

She should have died hereafter. Her father's will was not completely executed; her own—never shown to her mother—was unlikely to be duly executed, and the tidal wave of terror was already beginning to sweep across Paris with a surge that would carry aristocratic salvage to all parts of Europe. At such a moment what could happen to those three small children in Paris?

Not much is known of the private or personal life of *mon amis*, Prince Ferdinand. He and Charlotte were in fact remote cousins, having a common ancestor in James Sobieski, son of the great King John of Poland. Historians have found little to commend in his character. He was extremely proud of his family, and in his day arrogance and insolence were traits regarded as typical of any Rohan. The motto of the family was *Roy ne suis, prince ne daigne, Rohan suis*. As cadet in such a family Ferdinand long and eagerly sought for honors; yet in spite of his great pride of birth he at last, ironically, sold his name, as has been said, to a man of no birth—to Napoleon himself. One finds him, aged seventy-two, writing servilely to the imperial upstart on February 13, 1810:

> ... my existence is dear to me only as possible sacrifice to the great Napoleon: he is my guardian deity ... my probity is known; at my age one is not changeable ... your favors are the bonds, the indissoluble bases of attachment, and I await them with respect.

Two days later the awaited favor eventuated: Napoleon ordered that 12,000 francs be paid to Rohan "sur la caisse des théatres."

As a Rohan, Prince Ferdinand got ecclesiastical preferment early and rapidly. At twenty-one he was Grand Prior of the chapter of Strasbourg, and he presided over the rich Abbey of Mouzon. Among his greater places were the archiepiscopal sees of Bordeaux (1770) and of Cambrai (1781); he was regent of Liége for a brief turbulent moment in 1790, and in the last decade of his life was Grand Aumonier of the successive empresses of Napoleon. He was not content to be a cleric, a role probably imposed on him as the youngest son. In 1790 when the Revolution made religion look unrewarding, he wrote dolefully about his career:

> It is now very possible and even probable that I shall resign my archbishopric and go to live where and how I can, eating crusts—if they pay me the stipulated pension.... Just Heaven! what a reward after twenty years as bishop, and many more devoted *to a state or profession which has kept me from following any other* in which I might have had real advantages to be enjoyed throughout the rest of my life. With my brother-in-law much regarded by the King of Spain, I should probably have entered that service: I should have had real advantages and honors—*not mentioning an advantageous marriage such as perhaps I might have made*.[1]

Courts rather than cathedrals were his natural milieu, and his frantic unscrupulous drive to become a ruling prince was a very brief success in Liége, a success in which there was neither honor nor satisfaction. For him Liége was no glowing achievement; it was rather a ridiculous failure that cost him reputation and friends.

[1] Henry Sage, *Une République de trois mois: Le Prince de Rohan-Guéméné* (Verviers, 1909), p. 251.

By 1782, according to the *Mémoires secrets* of Bachaumont, Prince Ferdinand was "assez décrié pour ses mœurs." Very likely the trouble was his customary arrogance. The magnificence of his tastes would hardly be considered a blemish. He had built himself a new palace at Bordeaux; his gardens at Cambrai were extensive and gorgeous; a town house in Paris (Rue du Regard) and another house in Auteuil indicate something as to his scale of living. And there was also the *petit jardin* in the Rue St. Jacques. It was beneath him to pay debts promptly, but his income seems to have been generous. His young and wealthy relative the Count de Bethune-Charost gave financial support to some of Ferdinand's projects—notably that of Liége.

By 1794 Ferdinand and most of the Rohan clan had fled from France. What sort of magnificence he kept up during the years (1794–1801) when he was a refugee, we hardly know. Henry Sage says that during these years Ferdinand lived for some time at Pyrmont in Waldeck, and places him in Warsaw as of May 11, 1799. First, however, he seems to have gone to Italy. From Venice on November 22, 1794, he petitioned to be allowed to proceed to Rome, and he gives a sketch of his establishment: "I have with me only two clerics and my maitre d'hotel who serves me as valet de chambre. I live as cheaply as possible; for this business may last long, if even all is not lost."[1] The petition was granted, and in July, 1795, he asks permission to live near Bologna. His household is somewhat changed—he has one priest and two servants now, and in making his "petition to the Most Holy Father [he] does not claim financial aid: God be thanked, with economy he can still live a long time without importuning anyone" (Theiner, I, 435).

Sometime after his brother Louis, the admiral, had been guillotined (1794) Ferdinand wrote to Thomas Coutts, whom he had met earlier, suggesting that Louis had left an estate in the West Indies, near Port au Prince. The island of Haiti was then in the hands of the English, and Ferdinand wondered if Coutts might like to purchase the estate there. The Rohan family agents in London, he said, were Turnbull and Forbes. An émigré doubtless would feel poor, but an aura of opulence frequently graces Prince Ferdinand.

He might well have been *décrié* because of his obsession for women. Available evidence comes chiefly from the jealous letters written by

[1] Augustin Theiner, *Documents inédits relatifs aux affaires religieuses de la France*, 1790–1800. (2 vols.; 1857–58), II, 65.

Charlotte to her mother, where possibly a half-dozen mistresses are mentioned by name. While resident in Liége he received notice from an agent in Cambrai that a young woman at the château was *enceinte*, and insisted that she was going to remain in the Archbishop's house. The agent inquires, Is she to be allowed to do so? It is probable that he brought other offspring into the world besides the three kept in the *petit jardin*.

All told, his personal traits were those of the typical *grand seigneur* of the *ancien régime*. He was more ambitiously active than the type required, but he was the family cadet, and must struggle to achieve the desired magnificence. Blind faith in one's class (however derelict at the time) and contempt for unappreciative *canaille* and even more for unappreciative peers; rage at insult, even though trifling—all these traits were apparent in Prince Ferdinand. He was passionately fond of hunting, and could be seen hurrying from his choir dressed for the chase—knife at belt and gun in hand—and returning only in time to change quickly and conduct vespers. His impulsive violence on one occasion is alleged to have carried him to a murderous extreme. The chase having gone beyond the borders of his own lands, that fact was respectfully called to his attention by a keeper. "The effect," so Sage tells us, "was terrific. Maddened, purple with rage, Rohan fired his gun straight at the man. He missed, or merely wounded him, and drunk with rage, seized a second gun and finished the man." One can see why *grands seigneurs* were not universally beloved.

The Prince loved to live dangerously, but behind his hard and selfish personality—or possibly one should say *in front of it*—was another sort of person, convivial with men, charming with ladies, and, at Liége at least, acceptable to the *canaille*. He seemed to many a good sporting character. Physically he was attractive. Sage describes a pastel portrait of the Prince, preserved at Cambrai:

> . . . a pink face, with a pale, refined look. His forehead high and bare, his small eyes, bold and quick, suggest the elegant effrontery of a *grand seigneur à qui tout est permis*. His fine features marred by a chin which good cheer has doubled, show easily a faint smile, that of the man of the world. The picture of this agreeable, smooth physiognomy is a delightful pastel, white, gray, and violet; clothed, yet recently, in archiepiscopal robes, it recalls the look of Rohan as he ascended the grand stairs of his palace at Cambrai.

The attractive portrait—reproduced as frontispiece by Sage—speaks of a charm that doubtless made friends, especially among the ladies, and a sort of amiable emptiness that might be a weakness in public affairs. Discarded mistresses readily came back to him at times, and the persistence of Charlotte Stuart's passion for him during her years of absence in Italy attests his undoubted charm.

Such in any case were the parents of Roehenstart.

CHAPTER TWO

Early Years

One may perhaps imagine that on her deathbed, Charlotte Stuart confessed the secret of her three children and urged the Cardinal (in person or through an agent) to be charitably considerate of her progeny. She could hardly publish her shame and that of her family by mentioning the children in her will. She was evidently deluded in thinking she could depend on the Cardinal's generosity. Any late revelation of illegitimate offspring would doubtless anger him, but he was far from being the poisonous, melodramatic villain that Roehenstart alleges him to be. On the other hand, it is improbable that he was the simple-minded innocent that he has at times been painted. His behavior as to Charlotte's will was not acceptable to the Countess of Albestroff. The will named the Cardinal chief heir, and left a legacy of 50,000 francs and an annual pension of 15,000 to her mother the Countess. The 50,000 francs were "in favour of any of her necessitous relatives"—and that was the only reference in the will to Charlotte's children. Charlotte and her father, however, had little property of their own, and not enough to make her bequests practicable.

Clementine's pension was paid through Paris, and because of unsettled conditions she lost greatly through the rates of exchange. After 1797 the Cardinal was in flight from Rome while it was occupied by the French, and he was in no position to pay anything to the Countess. Her last years were supported chiefly by funds sent to her by Thomas Coutts. After about 1791 she lived apart from her grandchildren apparently, but before that time she had filled their minds with strong prejudice against their uncle the Cardinal-Duke. Prince Ferdinand in 1795 spent some time in Rome, and Roehenstart in a semiofficial story tells, with fantastic adumbrations, of his father's attempt to obtain justice from the Cardinal. One can only wonder how overt any such attempt would be.

We know little or nothing of the childhood of the three children. The two girls have not been traced at all, and the papers of Roehenstart give only tantalizing bits of information. Persons of irregular birth are frequently uncertain of just when and where they were born. The fact that Roehenstart tells quite needlessly varying stories about his birth may indicate his awareness of his illegitimacy. In his "official" Memorial of 1816 he says he was born in Italy on June 11, 1784. His mother at that time was still in Paris, but the date, though not the place, is perhaps possible. In 1825, when elevated to the rank of Commander in the Ordre de l'Ancienne Noblesse et 4 Empereurs d'Allemagne, Roehenstart sent the following data for his diploma:

Charles Edward Stuart, Baron de Korff, Comte de Rohenstart, Colonel de Cavalerie, Chevalier de plusieurs Ordres, &c, &c. né à Rome le 4 Mai 1786, au Palais Colonna, Paroisse des Stes. Apotres. Professant la Religion Protestant.

This birth date is negated by entries in the enormous diary kept by the Cardinal-Duke, which represents the Duchess as in the best of health at that time. Another year was suggested by the detail in Roehenstart's British passport (issued April 22, 1835), where he gave his age as *48 ans*. And his tombstone in Dunkeld dates his death as October 28, 1854, and adds "Aged 73 years." He was, then, born sometime between 1781 and 1787. Since he was evidently born before his mother went to Italy, 1784 is a plausible date.

Lacking specific information concerning the childhood of Roehenstart and his sisters, writers have evolved traditional romantic episodes that seem quite unhistorical. Two such may be found in the *Oban Times* for April 15 and August 5, 1939. They chiefly concern the connection of a Stuart lady with a heather grave on Campbell Island or on some other island near New Zealand. One passage from the issue of August 5 deserves quotation:

Baron Roehenstart's sister, Maria Stuart Roehenstart[1] was born in 1778. Both children were secretly adopted by a family in Warsaw named Ferguson-Tepper. Marie Stuart Roehenstart married Jakub Sobieski and was early left a widow with one daughter, Carolina Sobieski. This lady, Marie Stuart Roehenstart, is buried in the heather grave on Campbell Island.

The heather grave story, told variously by several authors, was given a lurid version in the *Oban Times* for April 15, 1939. No documentation

[1] The writer errs in fixing upon *Roehenstart* as a family name. The family name used by any sister would be either Stuart or Korff.

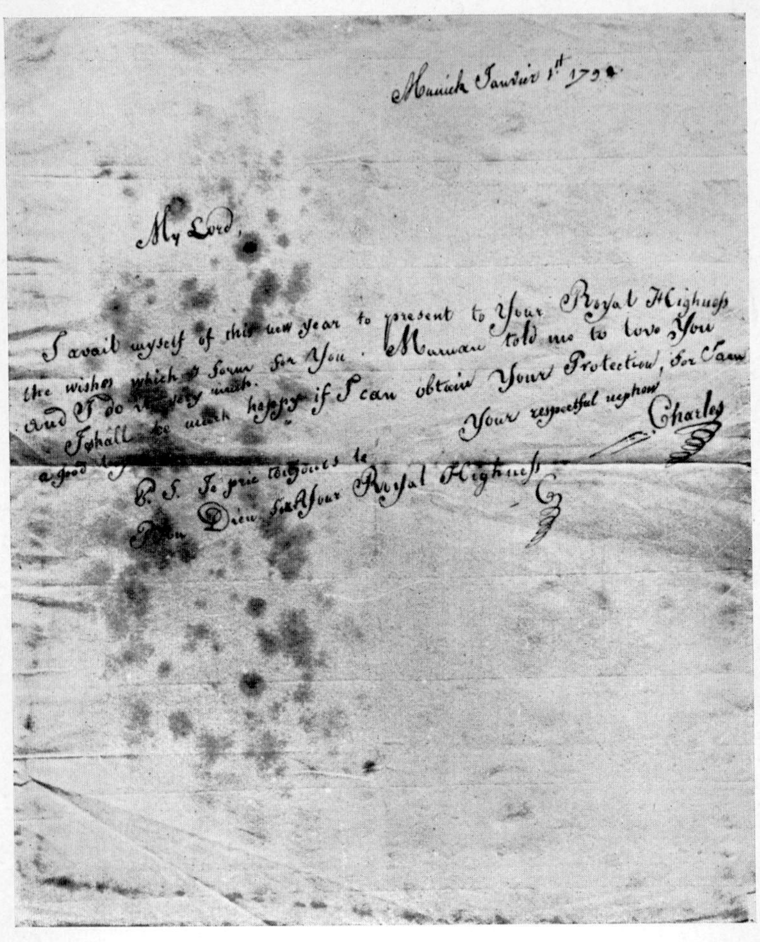

Munich Janvier 1st 179[illegible]

My Lord,

I avail myself of this new year to present to Your Royal Highness the wishes which I form for You. Maman told me to love You and I do it [illegible] much. I shall be much happy if I can obtain Your Protection, for I am a good [illegible]

Your respectful nephew
Charles

P. S. Je prie toujours le Bon Dieu for Your Royal Highness
C

Charles Edward Stuart (Baron Roehenstart), Aged 11 (?), Writes to His Uncle Henry ("Duke of York") Cardinal Stuart to Send New Year's Greetings of the story, which on the face of it is absurdly romantic, is offered, and there is no reason to believe that any of the several heather graves that make claims had any connection with a sister of Roehenstart. The story of the adoption in Warsaw is explicit, but again it seems impossible to make any authentic connection between the banking family of Ferguson-Tepper and Roehenstart. The family was Protestant, and Roehenstart was educated by Protestants, so he tells us. Their finances sadly declined, and if they adopted Roehenstart, they could hardly aid him in his later needs.

The evidence found in Roehenstart's papers indicates that throughout his life he had a "homelike" affection for the Rhine Valley, and especially for Munich and Baden. Somewhere early in his career he came to associate himself with the common family name of Korff. His full name with titles, it will be recalled, was Charles Edward Augustus Maximilien Stuart, Baron Korff, Count Roehenstart. Before 1816 he frequently uses as signature A. M. Korff, when not displaying his Stuart connection. It is certain that early in the nineteenth century a Count Korff von Schmissing lived in Munich, and while we have no proof, it is a plausible conjecture that Roehenstart was brought up in Munich by some member of the Korff family.

Among Roehenstart's papers all we have for the period 1793–1800 is four letters or four drafts of letters, perhaps never sent. One is in an untaught, childish hand; the others are in the excessively small but beautiful hand that Roehenstart had already acquired. Throughout his career he used both these hands, and in fact might qualify as a calligrapher. The first letter (in English) was designed for his uncle the Cardinal-Duke:

MUNICK Janvier 1st 1799 [or 1792/93]

MY LORD:—I avail myself of this year to present to Your Royal Highness the wishes which I form for You. Maman told me to love You and I do it very much.

I shall be much happy if I can obtain Your Protection, for I am a good boy.

Your respectful nephew

CHARLES

P.S. Je prie toujours le Bon Dieu pour Your Royal Highness. C.

The second letter (in French) is dated "M^ck^ Janvier ce 4 1799" and is written to his *Bonne Maman* (unidentified). It perhaps is written to inclose the letter written to the Cardinal, for it concludes with the remark "I send you the copy that I wrote to my great Uncle whom I do not love as much as I do you, since I think him very wicked. / Adieu, your obedient and good son / CHARLES." The other two letters, one dated June 22, 1800 and the other August 4, 1800, are not clearly addressed and are not easy to interpret. They contain nostalgic but vague mentions of childhood now past and are expressive of marked pain at being separated from persons much loved. In 1800 Roehenstart was sixteen years old or at most nineteen. The maturity of the handwriting in these last two letters is such as to raise doubts; but if composed later than 1800 they could not be used to prove anything. They do allow certain inferences. They are all written from Munich. They all imply a family unhappily separated and give an example of romantic self-pity common at the time and common in Roehenstart's later letters. There seems, however, to be a sincere sense of loneliness —of not being a part of a happy family group.

The vanished years may have been lonely: they were not idle. The boy evidently fell into good hands, and got for himself a very respectable education, with a strong Protestant bias. It may be noted that once in his later years Roehenstart called himself a member of an English Protestant congregation in Munich (see chap. xii, p. 128). The education was both practical and literary. His handwriting, already mentioned, and his facility in languages both would aid him in making a career for himself in some office of a great family—such as, for example, chamberlain to the Duke of Württemberg—or even in a business house. He kept accounts at times in a beautiful hand, and in all his writing he expresses himself more clearly and competently than do many of his correspondents, some of whom were persons of distinction.

His tastes, however, were genteel rather than commercial. He knew his Latin and Greek classics as a good schoolboy should, and he even acquired some knowledge of modern Greek. He had a good command of French, German, Italian, and English, and he probably had at least a smattering of Russian. He had a little Spanish, and even earlier than his rivals the Sobieski Stuarts, he undertook to master a few phrases of Gaelic. At times he wrote brief pieces for periodicals, and he collaborated in the writing of at least one book; but blood royal was not at home in Grub Street. After he failed in 1816 to get either employment or (preferably) a pension from the British government, he felt that he must then choose a profession from which to earn a living. In a letter of November 8, 1816, he stated his various capabilities to a friend:

With resignation I submit to my hard fate, and am determined, from this day, to lead a new life: "Vix teneo lachrymas, cum subit quantam jacturam vitae fecerim" and I will try whether it is not too late, by hard study and unabating exertions, to become, from an ignorant insignificant man, an useful member of society.—Three professions are before me: Commerce, the Bar, and Physic. The first I tried lately in America, acquired some knowledge of it, and really think I might do pretty well; but without a sum of money to begin with, it is quite impossible to think of it.—The Bar, my provoking broken English is an insurmountable obstacle to it.—Then remains the last, and most sutable of all. —Already am I not a pretty good Chymist, and also not without some good notions of Anatomy and of the whole Materia Medica?—to this I must therefore give the preference.—Tell me candidly am I too presumptuous in hoping that I may soon be "dignus d'entrare in vostro docto corpore?"—Next Tuesday I will set out for Edinburgh to study there Medecine.

These were perhaps dreams. There is, however, evidence that he did go briefly to Edinburgh to study medicine. Among the Hardwicke manuscripts in the British Museum (Add. 35622), Henrietta Tayler found an account of Roehenstart sent to Lord Hardwicke by Keith Milnes, who reported to his lordship details furnished by an unnamed young man from Stirling who lodged in the same house with Roehenstart. The young man read Roehenstart's Memorial, 1816, and furnished a sort of summary of that document to Milnes. He thought highly of Roehenstart, who offered to teach him French, and he admired both Roehenstart's learning and his wide knowledge of the world. The young man knew Mrs. Hamilton of Kames Castle, and, since she appears dimly in Roehenstart's story, the young man's account of her attitude (as well as his own) towards Roehenstart deserves quotation:

Mrs. Hamilton had him down to the Abbey and says he speaks French, Italian, and German extremely well. She has never conversed with him as to his family circumstances, but she cannot bring herself to believe he is the legitimate grandson of the Prince. If he may be believed, however, he is not only legitimate heir to the Prince, but the documents laid before the Prince Regent will prove it. Whatever he may be, he is certainly a most accomplished young man. There is not a language in Europe that he does not speak fluently and know grammatically. He is skilled in Mathematics, Logic, Chemistry, and almost every science. For reasons relating to him and myself I do not wish that any one should know that such a person is staying with me. You will therefore, I hope, refrain from speaking of it.[1]

[1] *Scottish History Miscellany* (1948–49), p. 129.

Such Roehenstart seemed to casual friends in 1816–17.

When this interest in chemistry and medicine developed is uncertain. In the Napoleonic period military life might seem more promising than science to a young man with a career to shape. The army evidently had been Roehenstart's first choice, but his military career is traced only in chance remarks that he drops. In 1815 he with a friend journeyed on foot from Milan to Geneva, and a very detailed account of the trip remains among his papers. Upon reaching St. Maurice he remarks, somewhat casually.

> Here the two routes to Geneva separate: the one by Lausanne, at the right of the lake, and the other, the shortest, goes through Savoy. But as the Austrian army had taken Savoy and since one had fought there, we took the longer route.

The remark can be variously interpreted. The Russo-Austrian armies had taken Savoy in 1799, and in 1813 the Austrians had taken the region again. In 1815 evidently Roehenstart preferred to avoid a region where "one" (he?) had fought, and certainly he was avoiding an army which he had quit less than ten years back.

Again, in his later travel journals, written hastily in English, we come across his account of an early heroic episode, of which he *seems* to have been an eyewitness. In June, 1833, as his ship sailed out of the Dardanelles past "the two shores where Abydos and Sestos are supposed to have stood," he mused in some emotion over the fact that Xerxes and his vast armies in 460 B.C. (his date) had stood on those plains; and with a sudden shift he inserts the following:

> Here in this very spot also in our own time did Mark Oates, the brother in arms & companion of my youth at the age of 15, with some chosen marines dash forward into the Turkish line and from their showy ranks dragged the green standard of their turbaned chief; from a remnant torn in the struggle Sir Sidney Smith had a small standard made which he forwarded to England, and presented to the mother of my gallant friend: how rich a treasure to so young a mother—a rich reward to so young a son.

Roehenstart would be about fifteen in 1799 when Sir Sidney Smith fought off the Turks in May of that year. It is possible that Roehenstart was present in the action. The fact would help to explain his recurrent brief mentions of an interest in the Turks, which lasts on till the Crimean War. However early his military career began, we have his explicit account of its termination. In his letter (March 20, 1839) to Mrs. Hamilton of Kames Castle, Holyrood Palace, he wrote:

At 16 I was an officer of Artillery, and at 19 I had on the field won my golden spurs and got promotion.—Immediately after the battle of Austerlitz I wrote a work on Strategy, which at the moment excited great sensation: I pointed out means of advantageously opposing the great warrior, and animated by youthful ardour & high feelings I felt that I wanted but opportunity myself to crush the Tyrant to the earth, nor did I find aught extraordinary in such confidence, for was I not the son of Heroes, the scion of a noble stock?—My extreme youth however raised against me a host of envious opponents, and I left the army in disgust.

This treatise on how to defeat Napoleon, if printed, has not been identified.

Our information about Roehenstart's early years is meager, confused, and in spots almost contradictory. He was born in Paris, probably in June, 1784. In 1790 or shortly thereafter he was removed from Paris, and before the end of a decade we seem to find him in Munich, to which place, if he was there in 1800, he may have returned from the Dardanelles. Presently, if not at once, he is fighting against Napoleon (whose courtier his father was), and after Austerlitz he bids farewell to military life. Just which army he left is uncertain. In view of his appearance in the entourage of the Duke of Württemberg not long after Austerlitz, one is inclined to think it was with Russian allies that he saw service. The Russians might fight as allies with the English in the Dardanelles and with the Austrians in Savoy and elsewhere. The gaps in our knowledge and the doubtful nature of some of it are indeed perplexing.

CHAPTER THREE

Russia: 1807-11

Roehenstart's break with the *servitude et grandeur militaire* in 1806 was definitive. We pick up his story in a letter from an amiable friend, De la Croix, who was employed in Paris in a government office—probably the chancellery of the Russian embassy—and who wrote to Roehenstart (November 28, 1807) sometime after Roehenstart's arrival in Russia in the train of the Duke of Württemberg. It is of some interest that he speaks of Roehenstart's being at Coburg. In part the letter (written in French) says:

> I received your letter from Coburg, likewise the marginalia which you added to those of the Duke. . . . I am waiting for details of your journey, and especially of your residence in a capital which is to me the more dear since it is that of my native country and the home of my best friends. . . . I am convinced that you will not fail to have a career in a land in which justice rewards ability and in which you will also have the protection of Monsieur the Duke and his wife.

The mention of the Duchess may be noted; for Roehenstart's papers indicate that he enjoyed perhaps a special patronage from her. Possibly through her, rather than through his military service, he was introduced into the ducal household.

Thus not later than 1807 Roehenstart is established in Russia at the court of the Duke of Württemberg. The Duke, younger brother of the Napoleon-made King of Württemberg, was generalissimo of the Russian armies, and governor of White Russia; the dowager Czarina was his sister. White Russia, because of the varying intentions of Napoleon towards Poland, was an exposed frontier. The removal of the ducal court from St. Petersburg to Vitepsk in 1811 was not for some of the court a pleasant change.

The Duchess of Württemberg was the Princess Antoinette (1779–1824), daughter of Francis, Duke of Coburg, and thus a member of a celebrated generation of that house. Her brother Ferdinand in 1837 became king-consort of Portugal. A younger sister became the mother of Queen Victoria, whose consort, Prince Albert, was son of the Duchess's eldest brother. Her youngest brother, Prince Leopold, married Charlotte, Princess of Wales, and years after her disappointing demise he achieved fame anew as King of the Belgians (1831). With Prince Leopold, as we learn later, Roehenstart had an early brief acquaintance. Among Roehenstart's papers in his best fine hand is found an eyewitness account (see Appendix III) of the Battle of Saalfeld (October 10, 1806), signed "Amelie." This was one of the Christian names of Duchess Antoinette, but she is not known to have been among those witnessing the battle. The account, possibly sent to Russia for her to read, was transcribed by Roehenstart. It is possible that he himself watched the battle from the windows of the château. An unnamed governor of Prince Leopold is mentioned as present in the castle during the battle. One may doubt if the account, a highly emotional story of the death of Prince Louis Ferdinand of Prussia, was actually the composition of Roehenstart himself. It is in any case quite possible that a connection with the Saxe-Coburg family led to his place in the household of the Duke of Württemberg. His place, that of a gentlemen in waiting or of chamberlain, entailed varied duties. He seems to have kept the family accounts, and when the Duke wished a considerable loan from the Rothschilds, Roehenstart drew up statements of requested terms. He was sufficiently approachable so that eventually humble petitioners might address themselves to "Monsieur Rénestart au Palais d'hyver" hoping for his kind intervention in their behalf. In these years, then, he might seem to be solidly at work on an advantageous career.

As part of his many duties, he paid the monthly pin money to the Duchess, and upon the removal to Vitepsk, he had her detailed directions as to where and how her apartments were to be arranged. He purchased music for Mlle de Buissy, who was possibly a governess, possibly a lady in waiting; he purchased the lamps for a new ducal *salle à manger*, and could even be asked to select ribbons for ladies. Later in his career, and possibly earlier, he frequently served as tutor or travel guide. When he leaves Vitepsk, his pupils are spoken of as regretting his absence. Evidently he was regarded as a person of intelligence and of taste.

He was skilled in what may be called, at a humble level, parlor games. This is more apparent in the papers preserved from his Italian sojourns, but even here a gay time at Krinki is nostalgically recalled by a correspondence folder in which he copied various semiliterary games. One is headed, "Bouts-rimées donnés par Marianne," and is as follows:

Vous voir sans vous aimer seroit une	Chimère
Plus qu'Iris vous etes jolie et	Legère
Vos attraits touchants inspirent la	Constance
Et l'amour près de vous marche avec la	Décence

Obviously a game like this, essentially innocent, might become titillating. More sedate would be a game of question and answer (here translated from the French):

Ques. What sort of music do you prefer?
Ans. Adagio: it speaks to the soul.
Variations are symbols of inconstancy.
Harmony: the sweetest should seem the voice of her whom one loves.

Ques. Why do those who most merit praise dislike to have people pay them what is justly their due?
Ans. They do not dislike praise, but they fly from flattery.

Ques. Why are there more unhappy than happy people in this base little world?
Ans. Because there are more fools than wise men, and because the word *happiness* is rightly understood by only a very small number.

In general these "Souvenirs de Krinki," from which these games are quoted, are melancholy. If Krinki is the residence of General H., who according to one friend wished Roehenstart to become his son-in-law, Marianne may, as we shall see presently, be the girl whom Roehenstart *should* have loved, but he was secretly devoted to her sister Evelina. Evelina is not mentioned among these "Souvenirs," unless by implication in the verses that concern the carving of love devices on trees. He enjoins one tree to "receive and preserve the oath of love which in spite of myself I was forced to make, and which she will never know." After the *bouts-rimées* of Marianne we find a formal farewell from Roehenstart, composed in English. It sounds fully as sincere as the passionate letters of farewell soon to be sent to him by her sister. Roehenstart wrote:

Honor, and happiness, and health, and comforts
of all kind may be with you, the most worthy of girls.
Preserve your life, and let nothing rob you of
those powers heaven has given you for your well being.
Once for all, adieu. . . .
Le cœur a dicté ces souhaits
et l'importune raison l'adieu.

The farewell seems respectful rather than ardent.

The most pretentious of the recorded fetes at the ducal court was the performance on August 28, 1809 (birthday of Duchess Antoinette) of *L'Auberge villageoise*, composed by the Duke himself for the occasion. It was a simply designed plot, concerning the marriage of the innkeeper's daughter. The action is enlivened by a succession of acts with singers, dancers, and even a tame bear. Roehenstart had a small role as a magician, and as such may have done some entertaining tricks, but that is not apparent from the manuscript of the affair, which he preserved. The sisters from Krinki were perhaps in the audience: the cast was drawn from the ducal "family."

Among Roehenstart's associates in St. Petersburg during the years 1809–10 was a traveler of some literary reputation, Messence, Comte de la Garde. He wrote songs, one of which set to music by Lafont was much sung in Russia. Messence left St. Petersburg early in 1811, and in 1824 he brought out a volume called *Voyage de Moscou à Vienne*, in which Roehenstart had some part. The volume pretends to be a series of letters to Messence's friend, Jules Griffith, who seems to have accompanied Messence on his voyage. In 1824 both Messence and Griffith were in England. The volume, which caused a complete breach between Messence and Roehenstart, gives much autobiographical detail, and Messence especially prides himself on the distinguished friends made during his early years in Paris and later as an émigré in other places. Of his Russian experience he writes:

I was in Moscou a year, studying its true type of hospitable nation. . . . I was two years in Petersburg, working to give a useful direction to *une association de bienfaisance*; but the results of good work that one wishes to accomplish are not always happiness for one's self. Surrounded, however by friendly acquaintances like Ypsilanti, Lapoukin, Rozewsky, Narischkin, Roehenstart, I cherished illusions which warmed somewhat this frozen region [1]

[1] p. 191.

The phrase *association de bienfaisance* is not too explicit, but from Roehenstart's later abusive comment, one assumes that it was a commercial undertaking. The *Voyage* represents Roehenstart as meeting Messence in June, 1813, at Budapest, as Roehenstart was proceeding to Constantinople. Since in June, 1813, Roehenstart was in the United States, the autobiography is not altogether accurate. The meeting was accidental, and Messence was much surprised to find that Roehenstart had quit his distinguished post in Russia. The meeting must have taken place after Roehenstart's visit to America (1814), of which an account is given in the *Voyage*.

By 1811 the household of the Duke of Württemberg had removed from the gaiety of St. Petersburg to the relative exile of Vitepsk. Roehenstart had gone on ahead to arrange the new establishment, armed with several pages of directions as to the apartments of the Duchess, who did not relish the withdrawal to the provinces. One bit from her instructions to Roehenstart may be quoted as showing, possibly, some tensions between the ducal pair:

> As for my own apartments I should wish them as isolated as possible, and if possible a large, healthy *chambre à coucher*, a *cabinet de toilette*, and another room for writing—with my ladies near by. Two large chambers are needed for my ladies and in addition one for my belongings. I wish furthermore that no exit—corridor or staircase—should be walled up or condemned,—a thing that always enters into the good arrangements of Monseigneur.

Does this last remark imply that the Duchess had a suspicious husband on her hands?

Roehenstart executed the royal lady's instructions with his usual high competence, and having done so he presently, and apparently very suddenly, left Vitepsk for St. Petersburg—probably at about the time the Duchess, whom he did not see, was moving to Vitepsk. To some of his friends as well as to the Duke it was known that he was leaving Russia for England. To most of these friends the reaction was an exceedingly astonished query, Why do you go?

Duchess Antoinette, whom apparently Roehenstart did not see after making the decision to leave, was both perplexed and annoyed. She assumed that he could not endure Vitepsk—and no more could she. The official story was that financial difficulties demanded his presence in England. That probably was in part the reason for going. We learn from a letter dated October 2, 1811, from St. Petersburg and sent probably to some port where Roehenstart awaited a ship, that the bankruptcy of one Sofniew, who was Roehenstart's broker or agent, was complete. In six months, so his agent H. Kramer writes, "The creditors are to get 5 kopecks per rouble. Thus I may get in your name five thousand roubles, which I may send you thereafter if I don't get an order to the contrary." In this bankruptcy Roehenstart probably lost a very large part of his mysteriously acquired fortune.

Kramer in the letter goes on to repeat what he had already told Roehenstart:

> You have acted wrongly in leaving here without conferring with H.R.H. [the Duchess]. She would have fixed everything for you: you know well what she would have done with pleasure; and if she knew the motive for which you have left her, she would not forgive you.

Kramer then briefly speaks of General H., who "desired nothing so sincerely as to see you his son-in-law" and of M. [Marianne?] who is grieving over Roehenstart's departure. Kramer evidently knew something of the emotional situation as well as of the financial, but he does not make it altogether clear at this distance.

One failure was not enough. A second reverse was said to be due to a banker named Forbes, who, Roehenstart tells us, had absconded to America with his funds. John Forbes was (or had been) a partner in the firm of Turnbull, Forbes and Company, once at 42 Old Broad Street, London. The firm was the English agent of Prince Ferdinand, who some years earlier had written to Thomas Coutts about a Rohan estate in San Domingo that had been intrusted to this English firm. Not long thereafter the firm went bankrupt (1803), and possibly Forbes had departed for the States. If so, Roehenstart might well follow him—even if a decade had elapsed. It is noteworthy that Prince Ferdinand and Roehenstart used the same English bankers.

Financial matters doubtless influenced the decision to leave Russia, but an indiscreet and unfortunate love affair may have exerted added pressure. General H. (of Krinki?) seems to have had two daughters, Evelina and Marianne. Evelina and Roehenstart discover that they are in love with each other, tragically, since the Czarina has arranged a marriage for Evelina with a general, and since apparently Roehenstart was supposed to care for Marianne. All that remains now of this affair are four excessively emotional letters of eternal farewell from Evelina to Roehenstart. She had gone to school to Clarissa Harlowe and especially to Rousseau's Julie, and had mastered at least the dialectic of love. It is highly probable that the moralizing Evelina represents the "unfortunate attachment" that was said to have ruined Roehenstart's career. He was apparently thought most eligible: he was no mere court servant. His social position was such that if there was a dinner invitation for the Duke, there was another for the same dinner for Roehenstart. The papers preserved show that he was socially desirable in any gathering. But if the Czarina was marrying Evelina to General S. and if the argus eyes that surrounded Evelina formed the opinion that she and Roehenstart were being indiscreet—if nothing more— Roehenstart's position would be jeopardized. In any case to marry Marianne and try to build happiness when her secretly loved sister lived near by would be torture—or scandal. There seems to have been no scandal connected with the young chamberlain's departure.

The Duchess of Württemberg also seems to have been very friendly with Roehenstart. One need not assume that the attachment was other than decorous, but it existed. We have already seen Kramer's opinion of Her Royal Highness's regard for Roehenstart, and still another unidentified friend had written to Roehenstart from Libau on August 20, 1811. The writer is doubtful about Roehenstart's whereabouts, but believing that he planned to take a ship at Libau, awaits him there, more or less as an agent of the Duchess, who may even have been spending a part of the summer at the seaside nearby. The writer of the letter (signed only "C de D") has waited at Libau for a fortnight, and tells Roehenstart that the Duchess wishes very much to speak with him, to know to whom she should give him letters of recommendation.

> She is much annoyed with you for leaving without letting her give you this last proof of her friendship and her kindness. . . . If you can possibly, good Roehenstart, sacrifice yet an hour for the affairs of Madame the Duchess: write, either to her or to me, what you think of Vitepsk. . . . Be frank, and fulfill the hopes so well founded of your zeal and attachment.

Evidently the Duchess—in a different tone from that of Evelina—wished to say a last farewell to Roehenstart. C. de D. adds a postscript to the letter already quoted: "I have just seen the Duchess. She again expects a letter from you. I beg you do not deceive her! She knew her affairs no longer in your hands. Have complete trust in her."

With very cordial letters of recommendation from the Duke and Duchess—which he preserved, and so perhaps never used—Roehenstart sailed from Kronstadt towards the end of September. His decision to depart was perhaps the most crucial in his life: he dimly realized the fact, and an undated memorandum, written down perhaps before he set sail for America, attests his mood at the time:

Father of Heaven! What have I done to deserve this misery? Why have I been, at one stroke, deprived of all that rendered existence estimable? Now I am bereft of all; I have neither father, mother, nor country, but am going to a land of strangers.

A more bitter reflection is included in a letter of late 1816 after he had asked the Duchess of Württemberg to send him some funds left in her care and she had sent no reply:

How unkind to behave so; the very idea breaks my heart! O vile vile world! I have not even a security—I am trampled upon by one for whose interest I have sacrificed myself; sure I have done for her what very few, and perhaps no man, would ever have done; but I do not regret it.

Thus Russia became somewhat mysteriously a firmly closed door which later attempts could not open.

CHAPTER FOUR

America: 1812–14

Once off Russian soil Roehenstart sent back friendly letters full of regrets to persons of the ducal household. The Baltic was unbelievable, and it took the "Susquehannah" thirty-five days to get from Kronstadt to Gottenberg. He reached London in November, where probably he hoped to find funds. At this time he seems to have had no idea of appealing for recognition as a Stuart. Before reaching England he said nothing about going to America, but various plausible reasons arose for doing so. There was the man Forbes, who, it is alleged, had run off to the States with Roehenstart's money; there was perhaps a knowledge that the Rohans had property near Port au Prince. Roehenstart when in America did visit Haiti, but it is extremely doubtful if anything could be realized from the Rohan plantation except by sale, and it was not at this time sold.

Our best information about this San Domingo estate comes from a letter written by the Duc d'Enghien for his *amie* (or wife?), Princess Charlotte de Rohan. This lady had in 1803 become the residuary legatee of her cousin the "necklace" Cardinal de Rohan, in whose castle at Ettenheim she had then lived for some years. The Cardinal and his brother Prince Ferdinand had inherited the plantation when another brother, the Admiral, had been guillotined; and upon the death of the Cardinal (1803) half the property was the princess's. Presumably the animosity of the Condés towards Napoleon would keep her from friendly relations with Prince Ferdinand, who was subservient to the Emperor. The value of the estate before the Revolution, so the Duc d'Enghien wrote in a letter preserved at Chantilly, had been estimated at 1,500,000 livres. "At the time of the confiscation there was arranged a simulated sale to the London bankers Turnbull and Forbes. These agents paid over with great exactness the revenues from the property, which was managed by their own agents, up to the moment when Toussaint-Louverture appropriated the plantation to his own use—an accident which turned out advantageously, since the property was thus kept intact even until peace was secured by the French expedition."[1] But since no returns had been realized for some years, the Duke hoped a sale could be arranged in the name of Princess Charlotte. Apparently no sale was made; for when the Princess died in 1841, her will bequeathed "A mes cousins de Rohan, mes biens de Saint-Domingue." We do not know what Roehenstart's relations with his father's family were, but it is safe to assume that in 1812 various heirs would be glad to have the estate in San Domingo investigated.

Certainly there were other reasons for going to America. Improbable is the reason given in the *Voyage* of Messence, namely, that a relative was sailing for the States, and had persuaded Roehenstart to go along as a part of a projected voyage to China. And it is conceivable that Roehenstart came to America, as many have done, because he thought it a good place in which to make a fortune. Before his commercial projects were terminated, however, he stated the moral of this attempt saying, "I never knew before coming to this country how painful it is to have debts." But he was more than a mere trader. His well-fused roles included those of tourist, trader, intellectual, writer, and lover as well.

As a writer he probably did little, but like many travelers he thought there were things about the newborn country ("whose birth," he says, "had not been the easiest") that his pen ought to tell the world. Before leaving England he had burst into print in the London *Sunday Review* (May 3, 1812) with a long letter of advice to the Prince Regent. He writes in a liberal, anti-Tory vein not always associated with royal Stuarts, hoping to "temper admonition with sufficient respect to make it palatable." He casually recalls to H.R.H. in one sentence "what were the reasons for removing from the royal seat that race which by *birth* had stronger claim to sway the British sceptre than any of your own family." Ten days after this wordy advice appeared, Roehenstart sailed from Liverpool, again on the "Susquehannah." Thirty-seven days later he landed at Philadelphia on June 19. His travels in North and South America were doubtless not so extensive as he alleges. He probably went to see Niagara Falls, and he perhaps traveled through parts of Canada. He says he spent several months in Mexico, but his

[1] Mlle Sardent ("Jacques de la Faye") in her *roman d'exil* called *La Princesse Charlotte de Rohan et le Duc d'Enghien* (1905) prints much of this letter, pp. 217–20. See also p. 381.

papers indicate that he could hardly have seen either Mexico or the northern coast of South America in the time spent in travel. One doubts even if he saw New Orleans, though he says he did.

As a systematic planner of travels Roehenstart drew for himself a freehand map of the States, squeezing in the Mississippi and even a part of the Missouri River as well as the Great Lakes and the St. Lawrence. The map, like its artist, was chiefly attentive to the Atlantic seaboard. It contains marginalia of some interest. Industry was uninteresting to him and is unmentioned. Colleges, on the other hand, were of interest, and he notes the location of colleges in Cambridge, New Haven, "Princetown," "Washington College in Delaware," and "Williamsburg College in Virginia." From some points of view he was an intelligent tourist. One assumes that the latter half of 1812 was spent on the Atlantic seaboard—with a trip to Niagara.

The early months of 1813 were spent in the West Indies. On January 14 Roehenstart gave twenty dollars as part payment for a passage to Barbados in the schooner "Republican"; he gave a promissory note for an additional eighty dollars to be paid on arrival. Possibly this was a usual method of payment, taking into consideration the possibility of non-arrival, since the British fleet was at this time blockading the Atlantic coast. Roehenstart evidently arrived; for late in February he was in St. Bartholomew's, and in April he visited Porto Rico. By May he was back in New York, possibly already determined to secure a ship and do some lucrative blockade-running on his own. He may have seen the process in successful operation during his first visit to the islands.

At a glance blockade-running might seem to any twentieth-century reader of American newspapers of 1813 a completely mad project; for the number of trading vessels daily captured either by American or by British privateers might well deter any ship from leaving port. But Roehenstart, encouraged, one judges, by Russian consular officers, was to sail under Russian colors, and they were somewhat privileged. Czar Alexander was thought by Americans to be "our mediator," and hence Russian prestige was up. Certain difficulties obviously existed. At the very moment when Roehenstart was purchasing a cargo, a leading Boston newspaper, the *Columbian Centinel* (August 7, 1813) remarked:

There are a great number of Russian vessels now loading in the United States with provisions.—Many of them probably are bound to British ports, and some possibly to the supply of the British blockading squadrons. As they respect the *United States* and *England* these vessels are neutral. If then, in the execution of Mr. Madison's *Embargo Order*, any of the Russian ships should be detained (and detained they must be if his officers do their duty), will not the Emperor Alexander, our Mediator, be likely to [protest]?

President Madison had recently issued an unpopular embargo order, prohibiting exports of provisions. The shipping interests of New England disliked the order, and the New England coast, while blockaded, was not very rigorously shut off. Hence perhaps New England was a convenient place to look for ships and cargoes—especially if one was to sail under neutral colors. In August Roehenstart in New Haven bought the brig "Betsy," whose home port had been Salem, Massachusetts; he rechristened the ship the "Alexander," proceeded to load it with a cargo of provisions—flour and corn among other things. He then set sail apparently for Jamaica, although officially he said for Havana—which port would not be affected by the embargo. The weather was very bad, but Roehenstart's troubles came rather from American privateers—Carthagenian pirates he called them. On September 3 within sight of Jamaica his ship was, as he says, captured by pirates. A more accurate phrase would be "detained by an American ship." In his Memorial of 1816 he gives a fantastic, romantic account of the episode:

The wind was favourable, and I was only ten miles distant from Kingston, when at 4 o'clock in the evening, on the 3rd September 1813, a Carthagenian Pirate came, took my Brig, and spoiled me of all my property.—The morning of the following day, they put me on board a small sloop, heart-broken, the edifice of my happiness entirely overthrown, and regretting not to have shared the fate of three of my crew, whom the Spaniards murdered at my side.—The loss of my collection is a more severe one than that of my Brig, since indeed no money can replace what I had:—bringing with me some Phoenician Inscriptions and Monuments which I had had the good fortune to find in a field distant six miles from Mexico! The Privateer gave us a very small quantity of bread and water, but owing to a fair breeze, we arrived at St. Barts before we have suffered much from want of nutriment. Then I returned to the United States 35 days after I had left New Haven: the strictest inquiries after my Brig proved of no use whatever.

There is clearly much fiction in this story as told privately for the eye, supposedly, of only the Prince Regent. Why Roehenstart and his men, put into a small sloop, made for St. Barts (some hundred miles distant) when within sight of Kingston is perplexing. It is safe to assume that he is making a heroic story out of his ill-fated adventure. The real truth doubtless was that the "Alexander" was intercepted by an

American ship, and was taken back to its home port of Salem, Massachusetts. There was in vogue at the time a system of ransoming cargoes, and within a couple of months after his return to the States, Roehenstart is busily trying to negotiate the sale of his provisions.

It is interesting to see what sort of *public* story Roehenstart—still romanticizing—was willing in 1824 to see printed in Messence's *Voyage*. The story is there told as if by Roehenstart himself:

You remember that I had long formed a project for visiting China. Not being able some years back to get a place in the embassy of Count Golowkin, I decided to cross over to England, from where ships regularly leave for Canton. I found at London one of my relatives, who, leaving for the United States, urged me to accompany him, assuring me that from there I should have frequent opportunities to continue my journey, and yielding to his insistence we embarked on the "Susquehannah" at Liverpool. In less than thirty days we were at Philadelphia: so near Niagara I could not fail to visit the imposing phenomenon of the Falls. Thereafter I visited Canada, its great lakes, and the majestic St. Lawrence. After having run about the United States, I passed to the islands. In San Domingo the court of Christopher presented sights the ridiculousness of which I could hardly sketch—especially when comparing it with life at the Hermitage which so recently I had left. From Haiti I went to Jamaica, and from there crossed to Porto-Cavallo in South America. There I almost witnessed the earthquake that entirely destroyed the city of Caracas. I then left for Mexico, where I stayed several months. Guided by the learned observations of von Humboldt I made a discovery the importance of which would have created in Europe a real sensation: it is that America was known to the Phoenicians, who had colonies there. I know that the difficulty of crossing the Atlantic without a compass has been objected, and especially in boats such as those of the Carthaginians; but to these objections I shall answer one word: I possessed sephulchral monuments of this people, inescapable proof of the fact I offer, and I even succeeded through patience and labor in transporting these fragments to the point of embarkation. The war had just broken out between England and the United States. Few ships escaped the pirates cruising the Gulf of Mexico. I returned to New York, and under a Russian flag returned to Porto-Cavallo to embark the results of so much trouble. We set sail in favorable weather, and were already in sight of the mountains of Jamaica, where I intended to touch, when we saw a pickeroon of Cartagena chasing us. At once I raised the Russian flag to show that we were neutrals. They greeted us with a full discharge, and a moment later I had twenty-five of these ruffians on board. All resistance was useless: several of my men were killed at my feet: I expected to be slaughtered with all my crew. We escaped death, however, but my rich collection of natural history, my manuscripts, my ship, all that I possessed were taken from me, and I was pained to see the funerary stones thrown into the sea—precious remains of antiquity with which I expected to astonish the learned world. Soon afterwards they put me with five men and three wounded on board a small American sloop which had joined them. Then without other provisions than two sacks of biscuits and a barrel of water, they abandoned us to our fate. The third day we came to Saint Barts; from there I passed to Halifax, where a war ship brought me back to Europe.

This first reverse almost cured me of the itch for long voyages; and as for China I came back from there long since. I am going to Athens now to study the Turkish language in order to travel through Asia Minor, in the hope of discovering ancient monuments in the Troad through the researches of my predecessors.[1]

These two accounts of Roehenstart's major American adventure can be in large part checked by his private papers. The Phoenician remains may be labeled "by courtesy of Alexander von Humboldt" who was a favorite author of Roehenstart's and who believed in Phoenician colonies in America. It is certain that in 1813 Roehenstart made two voyages to the West Indies: the first, that of a tourist, lasting about four months, and the second lasting for only thirty-five days. It is practically impossible that he visited South America and spent four months in Mexico—even that he saw Mexico. His Phoenician remains were useful in keeping the story of his voyages free from taint of illegal trade in provisions, and they appealed to his love of romance. He thought of himself now and later as in the great tradition of travel-writing, and invented much of his tall stories.

But he did buy the "Alexander"; it was taken and was convoyed back to Salem. Something like two months later Roehenstart was making efforts to recover something at least on his cargo. He drew up a detailed and doubtless inflated account of his losses, which, he found, totaled $17,899.50. The accounting he dated November 25, 1813.

His personal relations now began to be complicated. Early in 1813 he had become acquainted with Comte Gabriel Sampigny d'Yssoncourt, a Frenchman with some property in the States. In May he had borrowed $150 of Sampigny and in August $300. Such loans, to a man spending thousands at the time for a ship and cargo, were mere matters of convenience. But when in the autumn Roehenstart returned ruined by the loss of his ship and cargo, Sampigny became urgent in his desire for repayment. The two men apparently had lodgings in the same house, and enjoyed the company of ladies who perhaps also lived there. Letters that Roehenstart preserved show that the two men were

[1] pp. 425–28.

very kindly disposed to each other until this matter of the loans became critical. Sampigny wrote to Roehenstart during the first voyage to the West Indies in a friendly, frivolous manner, recounting the sorrows of the ladies (two or three of whom he represents as enamoured of Roehenstart) at Roehenstart's absence. Sometime, so Roehenstart asserted, he had repaid the first loan, but had failed to retrieve his written promise to pay. He alleged that Sampigny was now trying to collect that debt a second time.

Much of the details of this confused affair come out in letters that Roehenstart, after leaving New York on December 23, 1813, wrote to a lady whom he affectionately calls *bonne amie*, and who was Mrs. E. Chapus, 148 Reed Street, New York—a French widow with a young son named Eugene. She was among the ladies whom Sampigny had in May, 1813, represented as inconsolable during Roehenstart's absence. One passage will give the tone of Sampigny's early friendship. He is writing about the ladies:

Sobs and tears have had their way freely, &c. Would that you could make yourself invisible and come among us, and thus believe the picture that I can only sketch for you, and you would be quite convinced of the truth of my narrative. Your little air is the refrain of all that they sing or play. Nothing more touching has been heard. In a word, then, my dear friend, you do not cease to live in the midst of us: one Lady lives in the memory of what she was on the point of enjoying; the other on the hope of being one day the object of your attentions, and I on the expectation of the moment which will bring back my friend. Please don't forget the vow that I have made of consecrating to your service some years when you shall one day be in your glory. . . . If you have some need to regard my purse as your own, that will assuredly demonstrate to you, though very feebly, how much I should like to show that you are dear to me. . . . *Adieu, tout à vous pour la vie.*

But after the fiasco with the "Alexander" things changed. Even here the chatty manner in which Sampigny speaks of being in Roehenstart's service "when you shall be one day in your glory" doubtless did not please. Roehenstart never pretended to glory and he did not relish such jokes. In his opinion one gentleman did not hound another for money owed. These two attitudes are reinforced by a reflection that Roehenstart set down, possibly before he left Russia:

It is strange, but it is true, that those who have been thrust by misfortune to a state beneath their birth and expectations, consider themselves the object of universal hostility. They see contempt in every eye, they suppose insult in every word; the slightest neglect is sufficient to set the sensitive pride of the unfortunate in a blaze: and, alas! how little is this sensibility respected by the rich and gay in their dealings with the unhappy! To what an addition of misery are the wretched exposed; meeting not only those contumelies, which the prosperous are not backward to bestow, but those fancied ills, which, however unfounded, keep the mind in a constant fever with itself, and warfare with the surrounding world?

For his lack of understanding of this psychological bias Sampigny had to pay by taking abuse instead of money. In many of his travels Roehenstart showed intense irritation because of slights real or imagined from customs officers, the agents who issued or visaed passports, and all such people. The French Revolution might well, he thought, be instructive to the Prince Regent; but he himself clung, subconsciously perhaps, to the old idea that blood royal should instinctively inspire deference. If the lion knows the real prince, customs officers might be courteous to Roehenstart. Instinct, as Falstaff remarked, is a great matter.

In December, 1813, Roehenstart left New York for two or three obvious reasons. Sampigny threatened him with a lawsuit if the debts were not paid; and in any case he had to go to Boston to see about recovering something on the cargo of the "Alexander." During the stay in Boston, letters passed between Roehenstart and his *bonne amie*, and in them a strong *leitmotif* was hatred of Sampigny. For example:

Sampigny is a monster! I now have only $200 and do not yet know what will be decided in my case. I can give only the half. If you are willing to lend me $200, remit to him the enclosed note, and send me in your reply the money in two bills by the return post.—I don't wish to tie myself by an uncertain promise: sooner than four months I shall not succeed in repaying, but I will give you against all risks a letter of change on my sister in case I am not in condition to pay sooner. [December 27, 1813]

The startling thing about this letter actually is the mention of his sister, of whom Mme Chapus perhaps had some knowledge. It is the only mention of a sister in any of the documents preserved by Roehenstart. Sampigny was not paid, and Mme Chapus had lent or did lend money to Roehenstart. Upon his return to England he sent her a draft for $500, of which $200 were to go to Sampigny. Meanwhile in Boston or Salem he recovered something (not specified) for his cargo, and on or about January 23 took ship for Halifax. Before sailing he returned her letters to Mme Chapus. He kept copies of his to her, but not of the letters she had written to him.

He reached England on the "Raleigh" in the spring, and on May 3, 1814, arranged to have a sight draft sent for him by Rev. John Audain, Rector of Charmouth to an American agent, Henry Cruger. The draft was for $500. Either it did not arrive, or was unpaid for lack of funds in the Audain account. This failure to pay was unknown to Roehenstart for some years, and he regarded the failure to pay as the fault of Audain, whom he more than once berates for financial turpitude. The failure to pay must have annoyed Sampigny and Mme Chapus greatly. In his last letter to Madame from Salem, Roehenstart had concluded with "Adieu, *ch. amie.* I don't know when I shall see you again. . . . Never doubt the tender, living attachment that I bear you. Ah, how much I regret you, Adieu, *b. am.* My sincere wishes for your happiness will never cease."

During a period in 1823 when Roehenstart and Sampigny were reconciled, Sampigny wrote to Roehenstart that Mrs. Chapus was then living at St. Cloud, apparently with a M. Bosc. She was considerably more plump than formerly; her son Eugene was then old enough to have a mistress and a child, and it seemed a very cheerful *ménage.* If Roehenstart ever saw *bonne amie* after 1813, he left no record of the meeting.

One suspects that Roehenstart interested the ladies fully as much as they interested him. His fantasy was not love but position. He never expected to be recognized as an heir to glory or to the British throne, but he did hope to be able to live modestly but yet as might become a royal Stuart. America taught him that debts are painful. The ensuing years were to offer further lessons in frustration.

CHAPTER FIVE

The Tin Box

Early in 1814 Roehenstart landed again in England. While he was in the States, his father, Prince Ferdinand de Rohan-Guéméné had died on October 30, 1813, and that fact seems to have left his son more free to make frank inquiries about his Stuart family rights in his mother's estate—his "reclamations" as he liked to call them. It is clear that from childhood Roehenstart had been strictly forbidden to mention or to approach his maternal relatives. Now things had changed, and after having, as he thought, arranged the payment of his debts in America he turned his attention to an investigation of his family rights. He had no intention of revealing his true paternity or of pretending to any rights of succession—other than financial. Just as his mother, when in 1784 she joined her father in Florence, was certain that somewhere in the palace there was concealed great wealth in coin or jewels, so now her son was certain that with the death of Cardinal York (1807) somewhere should be lodged a great fortune that really belonged to him, but which had been seized by "the priests of Rome." Bishop Cesarini was in fact the heir of the Cardinal.

Roehenstart's finances are obscure. From somewhere he had a small income and usually, if he wished, he could pay debts (which are never large): like many gentlemen of his day he was frequently short of cash. He could not finance an expensive campaign against the "priests of Rome," but over a period of time he could persistently make inquiries and perhaps secure recognition of his maternal origin. He had certain leads. One was the hope that the Countess Norton, who had been lady in waiting to his mother at the time of Charlotte's death, might have information. Another was the hope that his grandmother, Clementine Walkinshaw, who had outlived her daughter by thirteen years, might have left documents of importance to his claims. There was also the widow of Prince Charles Edward, whom Roehenstart in fits of possibly acquisitive affection would later, on occasion, call his stepgrandmother. She was living in affluence in Florence. Rome itself might naturally have secrets to disclose.

After staying for a few weeks in London, Roehenstart turned up in Bordeaux, where possibly his deceased father, once archbishop of Bordeaux, might still have property. In August his letters were to be addressed "in care of Mr. Rougement de Löwenberg," in Paris. Roehenstart had got track of one P. Couppey, who had served the Countess of Albestroff during her last eighteen years, and from Couppey, Roehenstart got a detailed account of her extreme poverty during those years. Couppey had barely met the Duchess of Albany, since he entered the service of her mother on September 15, 1784, two days before the duchess left for Italy. He seems to have known nothing about the three "tender plants" left behind. Clementine, lacking other friends, had in her will rewarded the faithful Couppey by making him her heir. There was in fact nothing to inherit except that her pension from Cardinal York had been renewed six months before her death, and it was wildly possible that its arrears might be paid. They were not. From his grandmother, then, Roehenstart had nothing to hope for except perhaps documents, and the most interesting passage in Couppey's long and moderately illiterate letter was the following (translated from the French):

> If in all her distresses the Countess of Albestroff had not at times received some help from Mr. Thomas Coutts, Esquire, banker in London, who having learned of her misery had pity on it. He was indignant at the conduct of the Cardinal. Madame knew him [Coutts] very well in Paris with his wife and three daughters. When the tribunal of the District of Fribourg lifted the seals from the effects of Madame d'Albestroff, there was found a tin box [*boitte de fer blanc*] which contained a genealogy on parchment and some other papers, which a clause in her will charged her executor, Mr. Weck, former member of the Conseil-souverain of Fribourg, in Switzerland, to have them sent to Mr. Coutts in London, who was to send them to her relatives in Scotland. If any relatives existed, she did not know of them. She had no correspondence in that country.

In a postscript Couppey adds, "I don't know if Mr. Weck has sent on these papers to Mr. Coutts in view of the trouble that there was in corresponding with anyone in England." As a matter of fact, Mr. Weck had sent off six parcels of Clementine's papers in 1804, as he indicates in a drafted letter in French, which he turned over to Roehenstart in 1815. It is unaddressed but was clearly sent to some intermediary (probably a Mr. Haller, once mentioned) who could forward the parcels to Coutts. Weck had earlier tried to send on the letters, but they were returned, and he kept them, because, as he says:

At their return to me I opened one, and seeing that different persons could be compromised if they became public, I thought it proper to retain them until a time that cannot be far off. But the relatives of the Countess of Alberstroff being very desirous of having them, to whom they are destined by the will of the deceased, and I relying greatly on the intelligence and discretion of those relatives, I now decide to send them on in the manner indicated to me. I beg you then, Monsieur, to send them to Mr. T. Coutts. . . .

This letter suggests the way by which the letters from Charlotte Stuart to her mother reached the Coutts family, from whom they ultimately came to the Bodleian Library. The person most likely to be compromised by the letters was Prince Ferdinand, Aumonier to the empresses of Napoleon. Doubtless the papers also included unkind remarks about the Cardinal-Duke of York.

Couppey in his letter gives an account of the financial resources of the Countess of Albestroff, and says "I never heard of any diamonds sent to Madame." But Roehenstart was not satisfied with this ignorance of diamonds, and among his memoranda he writes down: "It is necessary to speak with this gentleman [Weck] to know what's become of a tin box containing diamonds, jewels, and papers relating to the Dutchess of Albany."

Since Roehenstart was much impressed by the story of the tin box, one might expect he would go at once to Fribourg, but instead he went to Florence to see the Countess of Albany. In October he sent her letters that she was pleased to receive, and she answered with a cordial invitation to come and see her. From this time on the lady and Roehenstart were ostensibly on friendly terms. Doubtless it was a matter of keeping an eye on each other, but it was more than that. In his travel notes on Florence, written in French, probably in 1815, Roehenstart devotes three pages to the society of that city in 1815–16, in an account which begins:

The first house in Florence for good society is without contradiction that of Madam the Countess of Albany: no foreigner of distinction fails to make an appearance there. Whatsoever may be her wrongs towards me and the bitter reproaches I may have the right to make her, I have to agree that she is a woman of great intelligence; but she is malicious and vindictive to a superlative degree. Her house is open every evening until 10 o'clock; she has a musical party on Saturdays, and a small dance for children on Sundays.

It was *chez la Comtesse* that the English colony congregated, and there Roehenstart met Caroline, Princess of Wales (whom he found ungainly), Lady Elizabeth Forbes (who was "beautiful"), and others who with the approach of winter migrated to Rome. Later, at Milan, Roehenstart (in French) tells us,

I went to pay a visit to the Princess of Wales, with whom I had had the honour to dance at the Countess of Albany's. Her manners are eccentric, her dancing is ridiculous and unseemly; but she is a woman of intelligence, who had not yet attained the celebrity that Bergami later gave her.—She lived in the Palazzo Borromeo, and was going to leave for the Villa Pini on Lake Como.

The society that one met at the house of the Countess of Albany was, then, distinguished. The attitudes of the Countess and Roehenstart toward each other are somewhat baffling. His later habit of calling her "stepgrandmother," possibly was a way of advertising his royal connection. On the part of the Countess we may imagine the attitude of an inveterate coquette. Witness the conclusion of the useful note (in Italian) that she sent him before he left for Rome in 1814:

I don't know the address of the Countess Norton. I know only that she married the gentleman whose name is written here above. I wish *bon jour* to Monsieur Roehenstart, and much good fortune in his amours.

The name written above the note was "Il Signor degli Abbati a Rieti," and with this lead Roehenstart was presently corresponding with the former lady in waiting of his mother.

He doubtless never told the Countess Norton of the fantastic document that he had fabricated in April before he left London. It exists on a leaf of octavo size and is headed "Extract of the Reckoning of the different Sums advanced by my Mother to her Ladyship Mary Countess of Norton." The Extract lists thirteen payments dating from January 3, 1780, to November 1, 1786. The total came to £2,350—a very pretty sum to recover. But Roehenstart clearly did not know that he had dated his fictitious payments impossibly, since Countess Norton came to Rome and to attendance on the Duchess of Albany only in 1788. In a letter to the Countess of Albestroff, Charlotte says that she first saw Lady Norton March 15, 1788. The two latest alleged payments set down by Roehenstart were as follows:

1786 May the 1st, by my mother herself	150
November the 1st, same year, by Mr. John Aly	150

Roehenstart's list is of value only as showing his imaginative powers and as showing that he had by April, 1814, done some research as to the bankers who might make payments to such a lady in waiting. Plausibly, Gouppy of Paris and Coutts of London are both named. The list of payments was never of any use.

Having secured the address of the aged Countess Abbati, Roehenstart wrote her the following letter:

FLORENCE November 7th 1814

MADAM:—You will be much surprised at hearing from the son of your friend, the unfortunate Duchess of Albany—I had taken the engagement never to break the silence which I have so strictly observed, but having been told that the Cardinal Duke of York repeatedly asked for me before his death, this reason could alone induce me to try to recover a part of my mother's fortune, of which I have been so unjustly deprived.

Often the Countess of Albestroff spoke to me of you, Madam, and wishing much for the honor of your acquaintance, I was ready to come over to Italy five years ago, when an unfortunate circumstance compelled me to go to America, from whence I am returned since a few months.

At my passage to Paris I saw Miss Brémont who knew you at her uncle's (the Abbé de Brémont) when you came to France soon after my mother's death. That Lady requested me to remember her kindly to you: as she was acquainted with my Grand-mother, I thought [it] advantageous to join her testimony to the act of notoriety which I got from some persons still living who have knowledge of the circumstances concerning me. Although my claims are just, still the result of the step I am about to take is very uncertain: however, I flatter myself that the remembrance of my poor mother will act upon your mind much in favor of her unfortunate son who has constantly been the sport of Fortune.

Fate has indeed contrived to pour on my head such a torrent of combined evils that my fortitude has scarcely been proof against them.

I long for the honor of paying my respects to you, Madam, and I hope you will favor me with an answer before I may take the liberty of assuring you personally of the highest consideration with which I have the honor to be

Madam

Your most obedient humble servant

KORFF DE ROEHENSTART

Post-office
FLORENCE

This letter, polite and correct but not altogether truthful—the Cardinal doubtless had *not* called for him; he had no act of notoriety, and the Countess of Albestroff very likely had never spoken to him of Countess Norton—this letter may well have "much surprised" its recipient. The signature is interesting. Up to about this time the signature is likely to be "A. M. Korff" or "Korff Roehenstart." Later he shifts usually towards "Charles Edward Stuart, Baron Korff, Count Roehenstart." One might have expected the "Stuart" to be used here. Surprised as she doubtless was, the Countess Norton, in spite of ill health, replied with only a decent delay; and the reply (in Italian) is in a square firm hand that carries conviction:

Excellency

Although I have been servant and intimate friend both of Her Highness the Signora Duchessa d'Albania and of the Signora Contessa her mother, I can only assure you with all truth of having been always completely ignorant as well of one aspect of the affair as of another, which you communicate in your most esteemed letter. I am consequently by my ignorance shut off from any way of pleasing or serving the worthy writer. My continual indispositions do not permit me to write with my own hand: therefore I beg to be excused. It is with esteem and homage that I do myself the honor of signing myself faithfully

Of Your Excellency
a humble and obedient Servant
Maria Norton Abbati

Ascoli 29 November 1814

This must have been a violent body blow; but Roehenstart persisted. Presently from Rome, in December, he wrote to her once or twice, and got at least one other reply, not preserved. He could not believe that the Countess Norton had never heard of his existence. He exaggerated her intimacy with his mother in the last months of Charlotte's life. On September 3, 1788, Charlotte had written to her mother (who had chosen Mme Norton as lady in waiting) commending the lady as *serieuse* and *scrupuleuse* and adding "As she keeps her eyes to the ground my Uncle finds her to his taste"—and so also did Charlotte. But at this rate the lady was likely neither to be told secrets nor to discover them. These things Roehenstart did not know, and he was obsessed with the idea that somewhere in Italy there was still another deposit of great importance in proving his right to his mother's estate. Most persistently he sought after any information the Countess Norton could furnish, and at last in May, 1816, he went to Ascoli determined to see the lady—only to find that she had died. He begged her daughter to allow him to scrutinize any papers the Countess might have left behind, but whether or not his request was granted, he evidently found nothing of use to him.

In December, 1814, after his early inquiries of "Queen" Louise and of the Countess Norton, Roehenstart, imitating English tourists, removed from Florence to Rome. He found all his key people either absent or dead, and so he cheerfully frequented English society in Rome, where he watched with critical eye the "school of waltzing" supervised by Lady Westmorland. He gently deprecated the English passion for the waltz, and noted that in waltzing Mr. Fazackoley sprained his foot. He had an audience with the Pope:

> . . . who, on my doing the show of kneeling, gave me most gently "*un bacio*" on the forehead. *Che gentilezza*! If he knew the reclamations that I shall perhaps one day be in position to make from him, if he knew all that I can publish concerning his good friend the Cardinal Duke of York, I think that instead of giving me a kiss, he would have sent me to the Castle of St. Angelo! . . . Yet one has to be quiet up to the moment when the protection of the Prince Regent permits me somewhat to open my mouth.

One doubts if Roehenstart at this time made any useful or permanent friends in Rome. It seems, however, to have been a pleasant winter with many new acquaintances. It is clear that to any sympathetic listener he did not hesitate to tell privately the story of his claims.

In 1815 he kept on with his inquiries in a somewhat desultory fashion. Then, as later, he could say with still a modicum of hope that he must be "content to go a-drift and expect the ebb." The spring of the year was tumultuous, with Napoleon back from Elba and Murat putting Italy in a turmoil. That meant that foreign drafts were a bit difficult, and in April Roehenstart (possibly to test her friendliness) asked the Countess of Albany for a loan. Her reply, refusing, was polite but firm.

Lack of funds, however, did not keep Roehenstart from going, a fortnight after the lady's refusal, to Venice to witness the ceremony of swearing allegiance to the Emperor; for Lombardy and Venice were now to be Austrian. Roehenstart spent something like a gay month in Venice. There were gondola races, balls, plays; and no one went to bed before three or four in the morning. The city was brightly illuminated, and Roehenstart comments, "I saw Venice in all its beauty." His comments on this sojourn occupy fourteen large pages of notes, but they frequently concern historical anecdotes of cloak-and-dagger amours.

By July he was in Milan and on his way to Switzerland, where he hoped to find papers of his grandmother, the Countess of Albestroff. This was a season when he felt like putting his travels on paper, and he has left an extensive account of his journey on foot over the Alps. The account shows his unusual descriptive talents and his keenness of observation. He shifts from one language to another, using English, French, or Italian as the mood strikes him. The journey, done in leisurely fashion, took him two or three weeks, from July 6 to some time towards the middle or end of the month—pages of his account seem to be lost after he leaves St. Maurice. He followed the route lately constructed by Napoleon's engineers, and comments on the sad deterioration that has been permitted in the roadway. He comments on the tunnels through rock, the bridges, the marble quarries—and naturally the lack of honesty on the part of innkeepers. He discusses the cause of the prevalence of goiters in many villages, and, more pleasantly, shows an appreciation of the panoramic views. He comments on the château of Chillon, "which was a state prison," and he is reverent and much aglow over the landscapes around Vevey (where he notes the burial of the regicide Edmund Ludlow) and he advises one to read the *Nouvelle Héloise* in the milieu of its supposed happening. A footnote, added later, indicates that in time he had outgrown Rousseau:

> Reflection readily shows you his beauties in their proper light, in which they seem indeed different: their warmth comes only from the brain, and, expressed in artificial phrasing, lets one see that the heart of the author was icy;—and then so much hunting for effect, of affectation of sentiment, that it is impossible that Rousseau really felt what he wrote. Doubtless many letters are admirably expressed, but everything considered I shouldn't care to re-read *La Nouvelle Héloise.*

His account of Geneva itself is lacking, but we learn from later letters that he did not like the town. In 1815 he made Berne his headquarters, and from Berne he planned trips to all parts of Switzerland. On July 25 he went to Fribourg, which he describes in some detail, much as an observant tourist might. He was especially interested in the château of Brunadern, which had recently been purchased by the Grand Duchess Constantin, sister of Antoinette, Duchess of Württemberg. He tried to pay his respects to the Grand Duchess, but she had gone to see her mother at Coburg. What one imagines was the real object of this visit to Fribourg is disposed of in one sentence: "I went to see M. the Counsellor Weck with regard to the Countess of Albestroff my grandmother, and I was altogether satisfied with his courtesy."

Returning to Berne after the day's visit to Fribourg, he begins to record his visits with the Marchioness of Bute, widow of the first Marquess, and daughter of Thomas Coutts. Roehenstart's first entry in his diary concerning this lady is as follows:

> 4 August. Visited Lady Bute, who invited me to dine with her tomorrow; Ladies Bute, Clifford, and Burdett have been almost brought up by the Countess of Albestroff, and nothing can render the painful sensation I experienced when her ladyship dwelt upon my grandmother's kindness to them.

This privately made entry exaggerates the connection of Lady Albestroff with the Coutts daughters: they saw her in Paris for considerably less than a year, but possibly Lady Bute led Roehenstart to think they had known his grandmother for a longer time. The exaggeration, however, is typical of Roehenstart.

He had several conversations with Lady Bute, but she was dissatisfied with the staff of the Falcon, where she lodged, and quitted Berne for Thoune on August 8. Other English friends remained in Berne, notably William Wall, who probably was Roehenstart's companion in crossing the Alps. Wall visited Mme de Staël, and Roehenstart later also paid the celebrated lady a visit.[1] On August 10 he went again to Fribourg, and records the visit in his diary as follows:

> I had written to Mr. Weck who very politely paid me a visit: I returned it the following day in the morning and I spoke to that Gentleman about the Countess of Albestroff's papers which were left in his hands: I had every reason to be satisfied with Mr. Weck's civility.

Here there is no exaggeration, for on August 11, safeguarded by written agreements, Mr. Weck turned over to Roehenstart the papers remaining in Weck's hands from the Countess of Albestroff, to the number of thirty-one listed documents. None of these really satisfied the hopes of Roehenstart as evidence. Several of them are not preserved in his papers: they may have been turned over to Thomas Coutts as evidence of Roehenstart's open-handedness, though why the Countess's copy of a letter from Pope Pius VI (October 11, 1784) addressed to the Duchess of Albany should have left Roehenstart's hands one cannot

[1] See below, p. 99.

surmise. The acquisition of these papers together with the newly formed acquaintance with Lady Bute completed Roehenstart's mission to Switzerland. He enjoyed the summer there and had talks with interesting people—among them Mme de Stael and the "famous Maret, Duke of Bassano"—and visited institutions that to him were very interesting, especially perhaps the "agricultural establishment" at Hofwyl. His records for the summer indicate his wide interests and his gifts of observation.

In view of the fact that Counsellor Weck had sent to Coutts, ten years before, the much-sought-after tin box, probably the greatest satisfaction to Roehenstart came from his acquaintance with Lady Bute, who before quitting Berne had given Roehenstart cordial letters of introduction to her father the banker and to her sister Susan, Countess of Guildford. In both letters she speaks of Roehenstart as the "son of the Duchess of Albany." His charm had worked readily with the lady but perhaps not completely. Lady Bute returned to England soon after meeting Roehenstart, and from Bath on September 19, 1815, she wrote to her father, Thomas Coutts, as follows: "I am most happy you approve of my having refused to lend money to Le Baron Roehenstart: he is a gentlemanlike man, very like Madame D'Alberstroff. It seems his mother, the Duchess D'Albany, married Mons. Roehenstart." The remark indicates a disposition to accept Roehenstart's story about his birth, but indicates also no disposition to give him financial aid.[1] E. H. Coleridge, who prints this last letter, also prints an undated document in Roehenstart's hand that lists Coutts's payments to the Countess of Albestroff from 1795 to 1802, and expresses the hope of making "one day to come" complete repayment. It would be interesting to know more than we do about Coutts's knowledge of Roehenstart's parentage. When (1788–89) on the Continent did he converse with the Countess of Albestroff concerning the grandchildren, who presumably were still housed near by in the Rue St. Jacques?

It is evident that by the time he met Lady Bute at Berne Roehenstart had invented for his further use a father other than Prince Ferdinand—his Swedish parent, Count Roehenstart, who will appear fully invented in Roehenstart's Memorial of 1816. One memorandum, if taken at face value, indicates that perhaps one form of this Memorial was first prepared for the eyes of Lady Bute. It reads (in French):

[1] Ernest Hartley Coleridge, *The Life of Thomas Coutts Banker* (1920), II, 333. See also II, 142–43.

I had never busied myself in putting in order the sad events contained in this memoir; and a strong stimulus, like the request that Lady Bute has kindly made me, was necessary in order to determine me to undertake so grievous a labor.—It is just as I have been able to write it in the space of some hours only.—I have reread it twice, but with that agitation of mind that makes one read without comprehending a single word: also I have forgotten to put in it a great many essential details. I have, however, been yet more moved to send it just as it is, relying on the indulgence of Madame la Marquise for the great number of unintelligible passages and believing that in this state it will suffice to give an idea of the nature of my claims.

Any memorial sent to Lady Bute has not been preserved. Such a history would be hastily written, but Roehenstart's habit of keeping drafts of such matters would be strangely violated if he sent her such a document without keeping a copy. It is of course possible that he sent her such a document which she, traveling about, did not preserve. It is hardly probable that in the summer of 1815 he had written the Memorial that was to be presented in October, 1816, to H.R.H. the Prince Regent.

For the late summer of 1815 we have no information as to Roehenstart's activities. From Switzerland he seems to have passed to the region of Baden and Stuttgart. In November at Strasbourg he received and preserved a letter from the Prince von Hohenlohe, whom he had known in Russia. One passage in the letter suggests that so far from pursuing his quest concerning Stuart property Roehenstart had asked to return to his former post with the Duke of Württemberg:

at Stuttgart. . . . I suppose you must await with much impatience the letter that will determine the direction that you are to take in order to be able to fix on a sojourn for the rest of the winter; for this wandering life cannot be agreeable. For me at least it would not be to my taste. But whatever place you choose, either in the north or in the south of Europe, I beg you not to forget that I take a considerable interest in anything that concerns you, and that you will give me great pleasure in communicating to me the success of your affairs.

He chose to go south, and spent most of the following winter in Florence. He made a hurried and obscure trip to London that concerned an "urgent matter" undisclosed. It may be that he considered approaching the Prince Regent through the royal cousin, the Duke of Gloucester. From a secretary a note came to Roehenstart under date of February 4 offering an audience with the Duke of Gloucester "any morning that it may be convenient to him [Roehenstart] to call at Gloucester House." Elsewhere Roehenstart remarked that he had been recommended by the Duke of Württemberg in 1811 to the second Duke of Gloucester, grandson of George II. As late as 1820 Roehenstart seems to have received a letter (not preserved) from His Royal Highness, but Gloucester never afforded the protection necessary to secure recognition for Roehenstart.

CHAPTER SIX

The Memorial (1816)

Roehenstart spent most of the early months of 1816 on the Continent, in the sort of wandering life that Prince von Hohenlohe had thought unpleasant. He visited Florence, Ascoli, Venice, and Vienna, spending some time in the last-named city. He had appealed to the Duchess of Württemberg with no success. A Venetian banker sent him £50 in May on the supposition that a credit on Russia for £150 would be forthcoming, though at the time no word had come from St. Petersburg. Toward the end of 1816 from London Roehenstart sent another appeal to Duchess Antoinette—with no response.

During the fortnight spent at Ascoli in an attempt to get sight of Countess Norton's papers, he may have received official notification from the Grande Chancellerie of the Legion d'Honneur in Paris of a new distinction. Translated from the French the document reads as follows:

PARIS 17 May 1816

I have the honor to inform you, Monsieur le Comte, that upon my report, the King on 16 May 1816 has deigned to authorize you to wear the decoration of the Grand Cross of the chapitral Order of the Ancient Nobility and of the Four Emperors and that of the Grand Cross of the Order of the Lion of Holstein.

Receive, Monsieur le Comte, assurance and perfect consideration
The Marshal Duke of Savente
Minister of State
Grand Chancellor of the Royal Order of the Legion of Honor
(Signed) MACDONALD

At the moment this may have meant little or much; later Roehenstart became mildly active in attempts to revive such orders, which had since the Revolution been in a sad decline.

Late in May he left Ascoli, presumably for Venice; in July he was in Vienna, where possibly he had some source of income. A letter from him to a literary lady of Corfu whom he had known and esteemed in Venice tells us that he had been very ill in Vienna, but that he was on the point of leaving for Prague, Dresden, and finally Hamburg, from which port he intended to embark for England. In leaving Vienna he had one of those trying experiences that were always so excessively annoying to him. In his luggage he carried some sealed letters. It was forbidden to take sealed papers out of the country, and to Roehenstart's exasperation the police insisted on opening and examining the papers, whereupon with an apology they sealed them again, and gave him a certificate to that effect. Small bureaucrats could infuriate Roehenstart always.

In Vienna he had been friendly with the Barone di Carnea, chamberlain at the imperial court, who spoke well of Roehenstart as an interesting person—"un uomo il quale aveva veduto il Ganges ed il Mississippi." It is fairly certain that Roehenstart had never seen either river.

In September Roehenstart left Hamburg for London, where finally he was to make a formal request for aid as a grandson of the Young Pretender, Prince Charles Edward. The appeal was made about the middle of October. Roehenstart's planned procedure was to ask for a personal audience with the Prince Regent himself. His belief in the effect of personal appeal was great; it had worked with various personages, and instinct might well lead one royal personage to recognize at sight another who shared the blood royal. But there was no readiness on the part of the Regent to grant such an audience. Roehenstart had to work through the numerous secretaries or legal agents and ministers, and his plans were thus totally upset. Everything had to be done in writing, and not with the secrecy that Roehenstart had hoped for. His request to a secretary named Watson, of Carlton House, for an audience with the Regent, made on October 14, was evidently denied. Two days later Roehenstart, as directed, stated his case in writing. This he did in the document that he preserved, called his Memorial. When the document was actually prepared we do not know. It is dated October 5, and that may mean something. It is here given entire, in spite of its length, exactly as Roehenstart preserved it in his own hand. Readers need hardly be advised against taking many details as having any connection with truth.

The Memorial

Il se fit un jour un alliance entre le
Malheur et la Fortune, et ce fut sur la
Famille des Stuarts que leurs coups
allérent frapper!

In the year 1746, Prince Charles Edward, during his stay in Scotland, took his headquarters at the Castle of Banockburn, near Sterling, at the Baronet Paterson's, who presented to H.R.H. his family, consisting of his son and daughters, and Lady Clementina Walkinshaw, his niece, afterwards known under the name of Countess of Albestroff.

The Prince knowing that the Queen, his mother, was the Countess's God-mother, and had the intention to attach her to her person, was induced, for this reason, to take a particular notice of her, and she being young, and of exquisite beauty, he soon became deeply enamoured of her, and that feeling was increased by a great service which the Countess rendered him, at the peril of her life.—Their affection soon became reciprocal: the Prince offered to marry her, and she consented to change her religion.

After the battle of Culloden, Prince Charles Edward, compelled during several months to wander in the mountains of Scotland, alone, reduced to a state of the most dreadful misery, and continually exposed to fall into the hands of those who pursued him in order to get the high price put upon his head, was at last too happy to go on board a small vessel, and to pass over to France in the month of September 1746.

Six weeks afterwards, he wrote to the Countess in the most pressing manner, and sent to her one of his Attendants with a lady to accompany her to Paris.

Relying on the Prince's promise, and following the impulse of her own heart, she complied with his desire, and went to France where she was received with all the rapture of the most sincere love.—They soon set out for Gand, and there were united by a secret marriage, 'tis true, but still the act was drawn with all the regular formalities. She was then acknowledged and considered in public as the Prince's legitimate wife. From that time she constantly lived with him, and then they took their residence in Liege, under the name of Count and Countess Johnson. It was in this town that the Countess was brought to bed of Lady Charlotte Stuart, whose birth transported her father with joy: He went himself to the Church with the child, and presented her to be baptised.

They resided at Bouillon, when Lady Charlotte being nearly seven years of age, King James sent word to the Countess that it was high time to think of beginning her daughter's education; the wandering & fugitive life, which the Prince was compelled to lead, being a great obstacle to this end, he desired her to leave her husband, and come to Paris where every thing would be prepared to receive them. Before she complied with the King's order, she tried a last effort on the Prince to induce him to consent to their separation, but seeing him quite averse to it, and having received another letter, of which Lord Alfort was the bearer, she thought that her duty as a tender mother agreed with this order, and in consequence left Bouillon, at 12 o'clock at night, on the 21st July, and arrived at Paris on the 25th.—The Archbishop received and conducted her to the Convent of the Visitation, in the duBacq Street.

This separation deeply affected the Prince who sent immediately several expresses, with orders to bring back to Bouillon his wife and daughter, and to make the best enquiries after them. But the King of France answered, that the Countess was under his protection, and placed in the Convent to begin Lady Charlotte's education.—King James wrote to his son to inform him that the Countess had acted in conformity to his express order, that it was a necessary separation, and that he would himself take care that his Grand-daughter should receive an education suitable to her rank. This promise was fulfilled on the part of H.M. who often saw the child, and was much attached to her. Sometime before his death, he sent Lord Alfort to the Countess to give her the assurance that, by his will, he had secured to herself a fortune, and also made a separate establishment from that of her father to his Grand-daughter.

Prince Charles Edward in the meantime exasperated at the state in which he had been left, and seeing all his efforts to recover his daughter ineffectual, had resolved not to see his wife any more, to whom he solely attributed the cause of his disappointment.—His brother, the Cardinal Duke of York, contributed to make him take such an unjust resolution, and the atrocious conduct he subsequently evinced is a sufficient proof of his hatred against the Countess, which originated in her having repulsed with horror and contempt the Cardinal's shameful proposition he dared to make when he first saw her.

King James died in 1766, and from this fatal moment the Countess's fate was sensibly altered. Her husband having forsook her, she applied to the Cardinal Duke to know what were the King's last dispositions in her favor. The Cardinal's answer was that from this moment he withdrew the pension she received before, and that she must be satisfied with a sum of 5,000 livres annually paid. "As for the will," added he, "you may rest assured that you shall never come to the knowledge of it."

A short time after, the Cardinal having formed with the Court of France the plan of a new marriage for his brother, and knowing too well the obstacle which the Countess was to it, sent one of his Agents to her with a declaration ready drawn, purporting to acknowledge that the Prince, her husband, having no longer an affection for her, and that the celebration of her marriage not having been performed according to the rites of the Catholic Church, she considered it as void and of no force &c.—The Cardinal insisted upon her signing this declaration immediately, and that, in this case, she should have a perpetual pension of 50,000 livres, including that left her by the King.—The Agent used the most threatening expressions to make her yield,—showed her a "Lettre de Cachet" to shut her up for life, if she would not consent by signing to remove the only obstacle which opposed the political marriage which was about to take place: in short he went so far as to say, that the Prince himself would declare his Daughter illegitimate!—The Countess who was of an extremely weak mind, was terrified, and forgot herself so far as to sign this fatal declaration, monument of her eternal shame; but the first moment of agitation over, she wrote the same day to the Cardinal to complain of the cruelty and cunning which he had practised: it was too late!

Who could ever believe that the Cardinal's answer was, that he was satisfied with her submission, and as she had signed the act of separation, she might henceforth rely on the exact payment of her pension of *5,000* Livres? thus cruelly and treacherously defrauding her of 45,000 Livres, having originally promised to secure her a perpetual pension of 50,000 Livres, if she signed the act of separation.

The new marriage of the Prince with the Princess of Stolberg was effected, and the means the Cardinal employed to obtain his views are well known. His brother, being extremely religious, could not be brought easily to give his consent: they availed themselves therefore of a moment when the Prince was intoxicated, a vice in which, since his last misfortune, he indulged too much,—they put a pen in his hand, and thus compelled to sign, He was much surprised in the morning to find near him, his second wife, the present Countess of Albany.—Seeing however, the evil irreparable, the Prince chose to be silent, and continued to drink, in order to drown his sorrows.—As for his wife, she did not even take the trouble to draw a veil over her conduct;—twice Count Alfieri was surprised by the Prince in his wife's arms, and the last time he would have run him through with his sword, had not the Count had the presence of mind to jump out of the window. Then she found it more convenient to leave her husband entirely, in order to be in perfect liberty with her lover.

The Prince who had always the tenderest affection for his daughter, which the Cardinal's dark & malicious aspersions had not been able to lessen, had sent for her: she lived with him; and by her virtues, attention, and tender cares, she was the consolation of her unfortunate father, and soothed his griefs.—He created her Duchess of Albany, gave her the Order of the Thistle, and acknowledged her for his only heir: the public Acts which were drawn in consequence are registered at the Chanceries of the Courts of Versailles & Madrid, and were communicated to all the Catholic Courts.

Nothing can equal the animosity and despair which transported the Cardinal of York when he heard this news, for thinking that his brother could not live long, he expected to get all his diamonds, which he coveted with great anxiety. He employed successively all the resources which power & money could procure, to oppose his brother's measures. The memorials which he wrote on the subject, still exist, and are more than sufficient to prove the horrible wickedness of a person to whom the Priests at Rome give the title of an holy man!—Perceiving however, that his efforts were without effect, he felt that dissimulation was the only means left him: his hatred for the poor

Duchess was increased to the highest pitch, and still he affected then, all at once, to have a great attachment for his niece.

The Duchess of Albany had married, without her father's knowledge, M^{r}. Roehenstart, to whom she was tenderly attached, and with whom she first became acquainted at Paris, where he came to travel through France.— His Grand-father, born in Bavaria, but from a Swedish Family, the Baron Roehenstart, Count of Korff, came over to England in the year 1715, and served in the English army; he afterwards left the military service, and married Miss Sophia Howard, by whom he had two daughters and one son, born in London on the 2^{d}. of May 1740.

Mr Roehenstart saw Lady Charlotte, loved her, and obtained her affection: he tryed in vain to persuade her to go to England with him, but as she would not consent to this, they were united, and being both afraid of the consequences of such a step, if known to the Prince, they waited a favourable opportunity for disclosing the *transaction* to him.—The Duchess was delivered of a son on the 11th. June 1784, and she soon afterwards confessed to her father her marriage. She not only obtained her pardon from the Prince, but he acknowledged his grand-child by an Act.—It was according to his desire that she sent from Italy her son to her mother, the Countess of Albestroff, as she could not possibly keep him near her, without making her marriage publicly known, and wishing not to give fresh cause of irritation to the Cardinal, they feared the effect this communication might produce upon him who had done his utmost to prevent her being recalled, and whose pride would be deeply wounded by this alliance.

Prince Charles Edward died January 31st. 1788, and the Duchess of Albany inherited his fortune, which chiefly consisted in diamonds of the Crown, amounting to a large sum.—Knowing too well how her Uncle envyed this fortune, she thought to have won his friendship by acceding to a most extraordinary proposition which he made her then: it was to make her will in his favor, and that he would, on his part, do the same, and appoint her his only heir.—She consulted however with her husband, who not having the most distant idea that her will would ever be of any use, and unaware of the snare, left entirely to her own discretion how to act, in order to please the Cardinal Duke, whose ridiculous pride was so far increased, that he had taken the most absurd title of Henry IX, King of Great Britain, Ireland, France, &c &c.—

In the meantime they agreed that the Baron should go to London to settle his affairs, and then return to Munich to prepare his house for the reception of the Duchess and her son, as they had determined to settle in Germany.

Soon after her father's death the Duchess had complyed with her uncle's request to go and live with him at Frascati and Albano. The Cardinal then lavished on his niece marks of the greatest tenderness.—But the unfortunate Duchess was all at once seized with violent pains in the bowels, and immediately left her uncle. She did not communicate her fears to her husband, but only wrote to him to hasten his return. She also wrote to the Countess of Albestroff, from Albano, in the date of May the 6th 1789, a french letter, in which she told her, that she was going to the Baths of Nocera, near Foligno, and added: "Si je n'étais aimée de tous ceux qui m'entourrent, ma chère maman, si je doutais de la sincérité de celui dont tu as tant à te plaindre, je me croirais empoisonnée! &c."

She set out for the Baths, but finding no relief to her unabating colics, she proceeded to Ancona, and from thence to Bologna, where she put up at the Palace of the Princess Lambertini. She felt so ill, that she was carried to her bed, and all the resources of art, assisted by the most able Physicians were unable to destroy the fatal effects of the poisonous drink which was given to her.

She wrote both to her husband and mother, stating the reasons which had induced her to make a first will in favor of her uncle, but that finding her approaching death unavoidable, that she destroyed it of course, and had made a second will, in which she leaves her fortune to her son, and that a copy of it should be soon forwarded to them: in another letter which she wrote again to her mother, two hours before her death, she says: "je me suis occupée, chère maman, d'assurer ton sort d'une manière convenable. Adieu, pour la dernière fois, les forces me manquent, et je souffre des douleurs inouis!—Recommande bien à mon mari, et surtout à Charles, de ne jamais faire aucune recherche sur ma mort. Je connais mon état, et mes premiers soupçons ne se sont que trop réalisés."—

Thus died the unfortunate Duchess of Albany, at Bologna, on the 17th November 1789!—I can not refrain from making some remarks on the manner of her death, although I am bound by a sacred engagement never to disturb her ashes by researches which would reach the illustrious name of her Family; but in recommending me to be silent, my poor mother thought she had secured her fortune to her son!—Several persons of the first respectability, and Mr Weck, told me she died poisonned: both my father and grand-mother were persuaded of this sad circumstance: I heard it confirmed at Rome, and repeated at Bologna!—

I have been to pray on her grave, and pay her the tribute of my bitter tears! —O my mother! may the tear of every feeling Englishman console your departed spirit! Heaven now rewards your sufferings.—Ah yes: this is a sweet and sacred idea which pours balm upon the wounds of sorrow, and saves from despairing of our Creator, supports, and makes us bow with a pious submission!

The Duchess dead, the Cardinal before my father could arrive at Bologna, took possession of all her papers, amongst which was her *second* will, which he destroyed, and being almost the Sovereign of the country, the whole of my mother's diamonds and fortune passed into his hands, without the least opposition.—My father however, soon arrived, and went immediately to Rome to see the Cardinal, and claim his son's fortune.—A most violent altercation took place between them, as the Cardinal told him that he had married his niece with views of interest, and that he might apply to the law if he chose; but my father whose feelings were cruelly outraged, reproached him with his baseness, and swore that neither he, nor his son, should ever make the least claims upon the Duchess's fortune, which he might keep:—at last this contest rose so high that my father was compelled to leave Rome in the greatest haste, being pursued by a legion of Ibires, sent after him by the Cardinal;—but he was fortunate enough not to be overtaken, or I think that no human power could have saved him from the Duke's resentment.

Notwithstanding all the repeated applications made by the Countess of Albestroff to the Cardinal to receive what was due to her by King James's will, as she was confident (according to Lord Alfort's assurances) that a handsome allowance was bequeathed to her, still it was with great difficulty that she could get a small pension of 5,000 Livres.—The Cardinal Duke, one of the first Ministers of the Church, had the cruelty, soon after the Duchess's death, not only to stop, and refuse the payment of those 5,000 Livres, but that of the pension made by her daughter's first will.—A man who carries the indignity of his proceedings to such a point is capable of every thing!—These facts are known to all those who approached the Cardinal, and I have seen at Rome some poor servants whose pension, left by the Prince and my mother, he refused to pay, and who bitterly complain of his injustice.—I have several letters from Mr Thomas Coutts, the Banker, with whom my Grand-mother was in correspondence, and, amongst other reflexions upon his inhumanity, he says: "The Cardinal Duke must have outlived all sense of shame!" The Countess died at Fribourg on the 27th September 1802, having before refused all my father's pressing solicitations to come and settle with him: she insisted on my being brought up in the Roman Catholic Church, and my father would never consent to it: she was for this reason much irritated against him.

When I received the news of my grand-mother's death, I availed myself of that event to write a respectful letter to the Cardinal, speaking only of the distressing state to which the Countess was reduced in her last moments: my letter is from Munich, April the 29th 1803, and I avoided making any demand for myself, hoping that time might bring the Cardinal to some feelings of justice respecting his grand-nephew.—My father, whose health was much impaired by sorrow, had forbidden me ever to pronounce the Cardinal's name, as he had taken a sacred engagement never to claim any thing from my mother's fortune.—I have however every reason to believe that my letter was intercepted by persons attached to the Cardinal, and whose interest of course was not to put him in mind of me.—I had no answer, and from that moment I renounced the hope of ever recovering what was mine.—The fact is, that, with my ideas, the education I have received, and the sufficient fortune I enjoyed, such a resolution might be easily taken.

I had before me a most brilliant prospect as a private Gentleman.—Attached, at the Court of St. Petersburgh, to the Duke and Duchess of Wurtemberg, whose Chamberlain I had been appointed, I was on the point to make, under their Royal Highnesses's auspices, a marriage which answered all that I could wish.—But adverse fortune seems to have brought me to a state of prosperity, merely to throw me headlong into an abyss of miseries, and by that fatality which constantly weigh'd with an iron hand upon the Family of the Stuarts, I was also marked to experience the bitterest misfortunes.—I received the news that a Merchant, Mr Forbes, in whose hands was placed the greatest part of my fortune, had become bankrupt, and was gone to the United States of America.—This was to me a thunderbolt!—If I had not been so foolishly scrupulous, my marriage might still have taken place, notwithstanding my severe loss, but I could never be brought to expose myself to the reproaches which might have fallen on me, to have been guided by views of interest; and this shocking idea, so strongly pronounced in my father, also governed me.—From these sad circumstances, I resolved no longer to remain in my situation: I left the service of Their Royal Highnesses; and it will ever be to me subject of the deepest gratitude, to recollect, with how much kindness they opposed my departure, and all the proofs of benevolence which they bestowed upon me.—Arrived in London, finding confirmed the news of my losses, and being miserable in the extreme, I did not hesitate to pass over to America, where a short time after my arrival at Philadelphia, I had the satisfaction to recover a part of my money.—I devoted my whole time to study, and travelled in the south to form a precious Collection of all the natural productions of that fine country.—I was on the point of returning to Europe, when the war broke out between England and the United States. My friends advised me to take advantage of this event to try some speculations, and I was too easily persuaded to this step, knowing the necessity of an independant fortune, and being in some measure compelled to it, having received in payment a pretty large quantity of goods.—The Russian Minister at Washington, Mr Dashkoff, had the goodness to give me a great facility to my scheme—I applied myself to business, and undertook a bold speculation which answered my most sanguine expectations.—Then I purchased, at a very low price, a fine American Brig, put her under Russian Colors, and sailed with a Cargo of flour for the West Indies, having on board my collection: my intention was from thence to return to Europe with Colonial produce. The result of this speculation was to all appearance extremely advantageous, and would have secured to me a fortune more than sufficient for my wants.—I was in the greatest haste to put to sea, for fear of the embargo law which was expected to take place at every moment, and I sailed for Jamaica, full of hope, happy, and planning the most brilliant schemes on my return to Europe; but how soon they vanished!—The wind was favorable, and I was only ten miles distant from Kingston, when at 4 o'clock in the evening, on the 3d September 1813, a Carthaginian Pirate came, took my Brig, and spoiled me of all my property.—The morning of the following day, they put me on board a small sloop, heartbroken, the edifice of my happiness entirely overthrown, and regretting not to have shared the fate of three of my men, whom the Spaniards murdered at my side.—The loss of my collection is a more severe one than that of my Brig, since indeed no money can replace what I had:—bringing with me some Phoenician Inscriptions and Monuments which I had had the good fortune to find in a field distant six miles from Mexico! The Privateer gave us a very small quantity of bread and water, but owing to a fair breeze, we arrived at St. Barts before we have suffered much from want of nutriment. Then I returned to the United States 35 days after I had left New-Haven: the strictest inquiries after my Brig proved of no use whatever.—I went to Boston, where I embarked on board a Flag of truce for Halifax, and from there on board H.M.'s Brig the Rowley, Captn. Hopner, and arrived at Plymouth on the 4th February 1814.—Soon after my return to Europe I received the distressing intelligence that, Two Thousand Dollars in bills of exchange, had been protested, and which I was compelled to repay immediately: with the greatest exertions and sacrifices I effected this payment. I had drawn those bills at the time of my last speculation, upon a wretch who had engaged himself to pay me at New York, on the 1st. May of that year, 600 Pounds Sterling in part of a sum of 3,000 which he had received for me, as a deposit; he used to pay the interest of my money with some exactitude, but I could never bring him to repay the Capital: he died leaving hardly one Shilling in the pound to satisfy his creditors.

Having been informed, at this most distressing period, that the Cardinal, Duke of York, in his last moments had repeatedly said that his Niece, the Duchess, was married and had a son, acknowledged by his brother, that he wanted to see this son before his death, and that he expired, continually asking for his grand-nephew, this consideration determined me to undertake a voyage to Italy, in order to ascertain the actual state of the things, and take all the necessary measures for establishing claims which I might bring forward. I confess I flattered myself that my Grand-father's Widow would be glad to assist me, and to atone in some measure for her past conduct; but I was much deceived.

I saw the Countess of Albany, at Florence; she received me well, and it was rather pleasing for me to hear that before I had let her know the object of my coming to Italy, she observed, and told me that I had a striking resemblance to the Prince, her husband.—I found her however excessively selfish, and notwithstanding her great age, she has not renounced her former habits: Count Alfieri has for successor a french painter, of the name of Fabre, whom she is said to have married, and who rules her entirely.—"Mon Douaire," said she to me, "est seulement assuré sur la succession du Cardinal, ainsi je ne peux pas vous servir dans votre affaire; après ma mort, je consens volontiers à ce que vous ayez tout!"—I have been besides inform'd, from good authority, that she wrote against me to the Pope's Minister, the Cardinal Gonsalvi.—This same Lady, whose conduct is but too well known, receives from the Court of England a pension of Two Thousand Pounds a year, generously granted to her, as the Pretender's Widow.—I have no proof against her; but I merely say that she was my poor mother's bitterest enemy, and warmly joined the

Cardinal to indispose the Prince against his Daughter, by whose death she also profited.—I easily perceived that my presence put her in mind of her wrongs which she could not have forgotten. When I spoke to her of the Countess of Albestroff's marriage, she made use of these expressions: "*Ah! on l'a bien attrapée!*"

At Rome I was detained for a considerable time, waiting with great anxiety for the Cardinal Gonsalvi's return from Vienna, where he was then at the Congress; but the Neapolitan Army advancing under Murat's command, the war compelled me to leave Italy.

The Cardinal Duke of York, I have been told, has not altered his will, in which, under certain restrictions, he leaves the greatest part of his fortune to his Agent, a Bishop of the name of Cesarini, who had a very active part in my misfortunes, and whose family, from a state of extreme poverty, enjoys now great affluence. The lands of Frascati remain untouched in the Pope's hands, and a considerable sum of money is due to the succession by the Court of Madrid. The will is in the hands of H.M. the King of Sardinia, the Executor of it, and is only to be opened in two years, I believe.—Poor Cardinal! what a dreadful situation must he have been in, at the moment of his death, when the remorses of a guilty conscience came to torment him.

In this forlorn and pitiable condition I am come to England in the hope of gaining some support in furtherance of my views.—My earnest wish is, not to give publicity to this very unfortunate business, out of respect for my Grandfather's name. But by merely proving that the Cardinal had no right to enjoy my mother's fortune, to show that I am the first creditor of his succession, and then I may recover something.—I am well aware of the great difficulty of bringing the Priests at Rome to an account, and nothing but a powerful protection can make me obtain this happy end.—In my distressing and forlorn situation, may I indulge the pleasing hope that H.R.H. the Prince Regent, whose generosity is so well known to all the world, and having granted a pension of Two Thousand Pounds Sterling to the Countess of Albany, that He will graciously condescend to extend his protection to the last of the Stuarts.

LONDON October the 5th
1816

This astonishingly naïve and melodramatic document drew its material largely from the fantasy that had been long building in the imagination of the author. The portions dealing with the early life of the Countess of Albestroff are almost verbatim translation from Clementine's own account of herself printed in the *Œuvres complettes* of Louis de Saint-Simon ([Strasbourg, 1791], XI, 144–59). Other sections may have printed sources as yet unidentified. Roehenstart had very little firsthand information about his Stuart relatives: the Korffs or whoever brought him up did not talk about his family. His prejudice against Cardinal York may be due to early prejudices imparted by his grandmother. It would also increase from the thought that upon his death the Cardinal had bequeathed his property to Bishop Cesarini, when (as a Stuart might feel) it should have gone back to the family.

There is no reason to think that Roehenstart gives a true account of the relations of Prince Charles Edward and Clementine, or that his lurid story of the "second" marriage of the Prince has any truth in it. Doubtless Charlotte Stuart's father knew nothing of her children; if the Cardinal knew of them, the knowledge came only from his niece's deathbed. She died of cancer, and was not poisoned. It is unthinkable that the dying Cardinal expressed a wish to see Roehenstart. The American episode of the "Alexander" has now been told twice. In the form printed in 1824 there is no mention of financial problems; in the form given in the Memorial, which as a document is merely a device for begging funds, the financial aspects of the adventure are stressed, even tediously.

From the Memorial one gathers that Roehenstart truly believed himself to be the grandson of Prince Charles, and that he felt that if the Cardinal and the unfaithful Countess of Albany got pensions, something ought to be due to a grandson. But he was no threat to the Hanoverians, and his pathos was too extremely proclaimed. His Swedish father, invented in such detail, was doubtless easily exploded by the Regent's advisers. His long covering letter, sent with his Memorial, which he naïvely believed would go straight to the Regent—and to the heart of that "sacred person" is painfully obsequious and flattering. It certainly did not help.

Twelve days passed after the presentation of the Memorial, and Roehenstart became nervous at getting no reply. So on October 17 he wrote a hedging letter, which still exaggerated his indigence. In part it reads:

> Rather than seeing my sad story become the subject of the public papers, since my Memorial has been given to H.L. the Secretary of State, I prefer renouncing my claims for the present, and wait for a more favourable opportunity, if there is no other way left for redress.—But reduced now in a situation of total despair, not by misconduct, as I can prove it, I will not make an appeal to Your Royal Generosity:—if you think however that the late Pretender's Grandson in a state of such a wretchedness, is an object capable of moving Your compassion and pity, I heartily beseech Y.R.H. to grant me only a temporary support to extricate me out of the horrible situation I labour under; its magnitude must indeed overwhelm me....

Other letters to court secretaries followed. In one (October 20) Roehenstart laments "being deceived in a most shameful manner by a clergyman [John Audain] who does not keep his engagement with me"; and in two others he expresses regret that his Memorial has been passed to the Secretary of State. One of these has, mixed with the customary pathos, some significant statements:

> ... the answer I got is "that my case and situation rest now with Lord Sidmouth to whom I must refer for the determination of Government." If one may suppose that I am base enough to bring forward such claims as mine without a just ground, then I have nothing more to say!—Too well I knew that I was not in proper measure to stand the present turn which my business has taken and never intended it should be so.... My whole history has been kept so strictly secret both by my father & grand-mother, that it appears indeed difficult to explain this enigma: still I have stated nothing but the truth, and a time will certainly come when more than my statement shall be fully proved.

On October 28 he was told that if he would call at the chambers of N. C. Litchfield in Lincolns Inn the next day he might have his papers back. Litchfield goes on to say that as for the documents mentioned by Roehenstart as supporting his claims:

> The documents are obviously most important. They are according to your statement in the hands of a person who could immediately produce them. It deeply concerns the interest of that person, as well as of yourself to produce them, the reason assigned for not doing it has no weight and therefore the production of them is considered as indispensable. I should not conclude without informing you that Lord Sidmouth is satisfied of the accuracy of the greatest part of your statement, but this must be considered to be the exception of that part which relates personally to your father & to yourself, which the enquiries which have been made respecting the Duchess of Albany do not serve to confirm, and of which therefore his Lordship waits for the proofs which you have to produce.

To this letter Roehenstart promptly replied with strange assurance: "I do say with confidence that in less than a fortnight I can produce the documents which I have told you I would deliver, and without which, I am well aware, Lord Sidmouth will not have the goodness to interfere in my favour for promoting my success in Italy." He would like £25 to relieve his present distress, but he paints a picture of his future financial resources that is far less grim than had before been given. On October 31 he got his papers back from Litchfield, and so ended the official appeal of Roehenstart, which, so far as we know, he never renewed.

His confident assurance as to producing his *pièces justificatives* in a fortnight is puzzling. He can hardly have expected to get anything from the Rohans. Did he hope to get the papers from the long-sought tin box in the Coutts archives? He was, during this visit to England, making himself a pestilent nuisance to the whole Coutts family. The four ladies of the family searched high and low, and produced (uninteresting) papers said to come from the tin box, but they never showed Roehenstart the box. A formal note from the second Mrs. Coutts dated "HOLLY LODGE; Decr 17, 1816," probably ended his aid from that family:

Mrs Coutts is ashamed and distressed that the enclosed letters have not been returned sooner, but illness in the family engaged all her attention and she really forgot them, for which she is very sorry and hopes to be pardoned.

Roehenstart felt so keenly aggrieved at the lack of real aid from the Coutts family that he meditated a suit against them.[1] He at some time fabricated a list of desirable documents, which included birth certificates, marriage certificates, letters, etc., not one of which he had ever seen or had reason to believe existed. They rather *had* to exist if he was to prove his case.

He had but little of the shrewdness of the imposter. His Memorial was clothed in self-pity and naïveté. His reiterated dislike of publicity in his sad case—which if his Memorial was authentic was hardly sad at all—is puzzling. One can conjure up hypotheses about it, such as that possibly he had been granted a small fortune by his actual father on condition that he never mention or seek aid from the family of his mother. More than once he speaks of the "sacred engagement" never to press his claims. It seems possible that his finances were assured only upon observance of this engagement. Such a condition would explain somewhat the secrecy he wished for in his formal application; it would account for his fear of publicity and his frequent later assertions that he could now do nothing but must drift with the tide and await a government decision such as could not be furthered by efforts of his own. A public application might thus in 1816 have been dangerous, and later applications suggested by active friends are at times discouraged by Roehenstart. This reluctance is puzzling.

[1] See Appendix I

CHAPTER SEVEN

Reactions

The Memorial produced no tangible results for Roehenstart, but it did stimulate reactions. Possibly it is mere coincidence that, after Roehenstart's appeal and his talk of documents to support it, the British government increased its interest in acquiring and transporting from Italy to England the so-called Stuart papers—the family papers in Rome that had been in the hands of the Cardinal-Duke of York at the time of his death. The purchase was announced early in 1817. More certain reactions after the Memorial are expressions by Roehenstart himself either in letters or in conversation.

Writing to remote friends in Italy he does not admit defeat. A sentence from a letter to his Venetian friend the Countess Petrettini may illustrate this mood: "I have had at Carlton House a gracious audience in which I have presented my Memorial, which has made here, I shall not say a *furor*, but a fairly great sensation." The gracious audience was only with General Bloomfield, gentleman in waiting to the Regent, and the sensation was chiefly felt by Roehenstart himself. A week after writing to this countess he sent a long letter to his friend William [Wall?], who had been his companion in the journey to Switzerland in 1815. This letter, though long, seems worth giving in its entirety:

LONDON Friday 8th November 1816

MY DEAR WILLIAM,

I would have written to you before this, had I something new to communicate respecting a business in which I know you take a great interest.—Already you have heard my going to Carlton House, to see G.al Bloomfield, and present my Memorial. I said to that Gentleman I thought such an open candid application was more likely to ensure me success, than if I had looked for protectors amongst some persons of high rank whom I named to him. The fact is, I was deeply affected not to be enabled to follow up the plan I had fixed upon, and the unworthy Rector of Chermouth having so shamefully deceived and cheated me out of my £225, I was all at once thrown off my guard, and not having any more money, I could not muster courage enough to wait upon the Duke of Gloucester, to whom I have been strongly recommended 5 years ago by his particular friend the Duke of Wurtemberg. One feels indeed very stupid sans argent, and I could neither afford making the expenses of dress & carriages to go and see Prince Leopold, who, I do not think, would have taken up my business, by reason of policy, but whose acquaintance with me, might have at least given some countenance to my personal character.—I could never succeed in getting an audience from the Prince Regent, and I was confident, as I am still now, that only *two words* I should have said to him, were sufficient to interest him strongly in my favour.—You know, dear friend, what I have refused!—I never did, nor shall I ever regret it; not by any means from consideration of personal safety,—no sure! many times have I not affronted dangers and death with pleasure? I never knew what fear is;—but I acted by this principle, that I found the step totally unjust.—Even at this moment, forlorn as I am, and poorer than a rat, I do pride [*sic*] in having done so, notwithstanding the bitter consequences of my refusal, and from my own approbation I derive a pleasure far superior to what rank or riches could have procured me.—In short after having been several times to C[arlton] H[ouse], my papers were sent by Mr Watson to Lord Sidmouth:—this distresses me much, as they were intended for the Prince alone, and the idea of any publicity of my sad story, makes me shudder!—His Lordship I must say, has been polite to me, & appointed two Sollicitors for the investigation of my business; but they sat down with the resolution, I may think it, of embroiling a case, which, I am aware, is already too obscure & extraordinary by itself.—Tired of their postponing, I requested to know all at once whether I could expect something should be done for me, observing at the same time that I put myself in their power, quite unprotected, and that I was most desirous to make as clear as daylight the points to which they might object. I went even so far as to say & write, that, if Lord Sidmouth would deal with me with kindness, I would engage to prove *more* than my statement: this I can easily do!—The answer I got at last from White-Hall was that I must wait for the decision of Government, which could not be given so soon on a case of such an important nature.—To this I represented that I was in the painful necessity of applying for support, proving that, from a large sum of money which is owed to me in Russia, 60,000 francs at Paris, and several other small sums, I could not get one single shilling.—The very day of my application, came a servant from the Treasury, who, with much noise and a loud knock at my door, delivered me a letter which contained an order for money to the amount of—I will not tell it you, for I feel too ashamed of it!—I confess that I opened the letter with the firm persuasion that it contained a good round sum, and never felt so much disappointed in my life.—Is this the so much talked of vaunted generosity?—

Shame! what a shabby offer! I immediately refused it with a feeling of pride I could not repress, and went on with a train of remarks which I now think might have very well secured me a place, amongst or near wild beasts, in that ancient Palace which Julius Caesar is said to have originally built.—My letter has been answered without a new offer, and it shows me that they are irritated at my refusal.—Such stands the business now, I must suffer, and prudence bids me to hold my tongue.—

If I could go decently to Russia, and not like a starved beggar, I am sure the Dutchess would interest the Emperor on my behalf; but old John Bull is not likely to be much influenced by these means. I might also either take back my situation, or at least get an advantageous one:—'tis better not to think any more of Courts which I hate.—Since my arrival in London I wrote again to the Princess, begging she would send me a small part of my money: I have no answer: how unkind to behave so; the very idea breaks my heart! O vile, vile world! I have not even a security,—I am trampled upon by one for whose interest I have sacrificed myself; sure I have done for her what very few, and perhaps no man, would ever have done; but I do not regret it.—

The exigency of my cruel situation prevents absolutely my going after my money, to try to obtain some redress, and after to look for a protector to promote my claims.—I should be happy if I had seen the Prince Regent: his smiles would have raised my sinking hopes, and now H.R.H. appears to look upon me much like the D.—"with the ghastly smile of an horrible grin."—But no matter! I am become a philosopher, and despair won't do. I shall have a resource in Providence, and perhaps Dame Fortune may at last grant me her favours when I least expect them.

I know, dear William, you will laugh at my project, but I made up my mind, & will not hesitate submitting it to you, as to one good generous friend who has already so kindly proved me he felt some sympathy for my sorrows.—With resignation I submit to my hard fate, and am determined, from this day, to lead on a new life: "Vix teneo lachrymas, cum subit quantam jacturam vitae fecerim" and I will try whether it is not too late, by hard study and unabating exertions, to become, from an ignorant insignificant man, an useful member of society.—Three professions are before me: Commerce, the Bar, and Physic. The first I tried lately in America, acquired some knowledge of it, and really think I might do pretty well; but without a sum of money to begin with, it is quite impossible to think of it.—The Bar, my provoking broken English is an insurmountable obstacle to it.—There remains the last, and most sutable of all.—Already am I not a pretty good Chymist, and also not without some good notions of Anatomy and of the whole Materia Medica?—to this I must therefore give the preference.—Tell me candidly am I too presumptuous in hoping that I may soon be "dignus d'entrare in vostro docto corpore?"—Next Tuesday I will set out for Edinburgh to study there Medicine. I do not think to leave London with more than £40, but I expect receiving shortly some money, and should this fail, I shall give lessons during the day, and study in the night.—Almost all the languages of Europe, the English excepted, I do speak and write them well, and after all I will do what I can to earn my bread, since I am come to this extremity. I don't think that Government will make any step in my favour, and if I can have strength of mind to rely upon myself, & sufficient energy to exert my abilities, I may become independent. Such is my determined plan. You would confer a great obligation upon me, my good friend, if you could have the kindness to forward me, by return of the Mail, a letter of introduction to some Physician in Edinburgh, who would take me under his patronage,—

I awake now after a long dream, and I must absolutely forget all my pompous claims, which however may be one day supported: pray mind that I allude only to Frascati, and the Pension of Government!—I hope Heaven will grant me courage and perseverance to go through my new undertaking, and I shall find at least some consolation in the idea that extravagance has not lead me to distress:—never have I been guilty of any dishonourable action, and except the foolish waste of my time, which I most bitterly regret, I have a tolerable good opinion of myself.—I am no builder of Castle [*sic*] in the air, and shall not leave the field without a fair trial; if I must give it up, then for last resource I'll fight my way back to—do not laugh at me William, to—la mia cara Principessa Indiana!—She is indeed the finest girl I ever saw in my life, as good as true & sincere in her attachment to me.—Pray recollect what I told you of her: is it not very singular? She assured me, when we parted, that she had not the least doubt, but she should see me again: she said she knew I loved her, and protested she would never marry any man but me.—Here listen to my Logic!—Her good old father being dead, she must be the Queen, and then your humble servant shall be of course His Majesty.—Enough with my nonsense!—

All what I look for at this moment of wretchedness is, not a Crown, but to get my bread in Scotland.—Water & a crust of bread in that country, so endeared to me by so many sad & tender recollections, the theme of my infancy, will be more pleasing than all the luxuries to which I have been used till these last years.—My mind is now almost easy, and after all I think that, things which cannot change for the worse, must infallibly one day or an other, change for the better.—So let that vile woman, who enjoys the undeserved generosity of Government, be happy, if she can be so, in speaking against me; —let all the infernal set of priests at Rome warmly join her.—I have stated nothing but the truth: Honour & Virtue I will never forfeit,—and I despise those wretches who wish to deprive me of them. My conscience is my only comfort, and as long as I'll have it for a friend, I will hope for a better time.—I I am certain that if the Prince knew me, or at least if he had heard what I could say & prove to him, he would do me justice; but I assure you, had I not lost my Brig & all I possessed, I should have religiously kept my engagement, and never said a word about my claims.—But I must put a stop to my long letter, which, were I not certain of your friendship, I would say ought to have tired you.

Frattanto addio di tutto cuore, pregiatissimo mio amico,

I am forever,

Yours most faithfully

This seems to be an unusually honest and courageous letter. One must, of course, doubt if having asked for £25, Roehenstart refused with contempt the small offer actually made him. One notes with interest and bewilderment his mention of Princess Antoinette of Württemberg. But at several points Roehenstart seems to have his feet firmly planted in reality—though he readily darts off to the fantasy of an American Indian princess, who would readily make him a king. . . .

He did not sink inactive into despair. On "next Tuesday" he did actually go to Edinburgh and commence, briefly, the study of medicine. Interesting record of this visit—unmentioned in his personal papers—was found by the late Henrietta Tayler among the Hardwicke manuscripts in the British Museum. Letters from Keith Milnes to Philip, third Earl of Hardwicke, give impressions of Roehenstart reported to Milnes by a young student who lodged in the same house with Roehenstart. Without the alleged reserve Roehenstart spoke of his claims, and allowed his new-found friend to read the Memorial. The young Scot (unnamed) was fascinated by Roehenstart's wide experience of life in many lands and by his charming personality. The details recalled from the Memorial are somewhat inaccurate, but the letters give an excellent account of Roehenstart's character and education. Our hero remained in Edinburgh possibly for two months. He then left—no reason given—planning to cross to Paris and then to proceed to St. Petersburg and beg for Russian intervention in support of his claims.

He did not eventually go to Russia, but he did at times, possibly as late as 1825, hope that friends in that country would exercise influence in his behalf. He also solicited the support of various German princes. A letter from the Chancellor of the Duke of Württemberg, Starynkewitch, agreed to further Roehenstart's claims in 1825, if Roehenstart would send "without the least delay . . . copies of papers which seem to you indispensable in proving the validity of these titles." The sad truth of course was that Roehenstart had no papers such as he more than once boasted of having.

The strangest reaction to the Memorial came in the summer of 1817. Roehenstart had apparently spent six months in Paris after quitting the study of medicine. He says he saw Lord Sidmouth when passing through London on his way to the Continent, and his lordship evidently thought it worth while to keep an eye on Roehenstart. The British government asked one of its secret agents in Paris, who was, as it turned out, also a secret agent of the French police, to furnish some report on the conduct and activities of Roehenstart. This agent, John Schrader, persuaded a young Prussian officer, whose arrest for theft Roehenstart had caused, to make vague charges to the effect that Roehenstart was commissioning an army for the invasion of England. No less than that! Evidently Schrader thought that with such charges he should rate a distinguished promotion at least.

Imagine Roehenstart's astonishment when on July 3, 1817, he received a summons from the Ministère de Police Générale to present himself the next day in order to clear up an affair not described in the summons. Informed of the charge against him, Roehenstart immediately appealed to the British ambassador, Sir Charles Stuart, to whom he had in April sent a copy of the Memorial. Roehenstart protests his innocence, and resents having charges, made against him by a felon, taken seriously. He protests his loyalty to the Prince Regent: "I solemnly declare that no man can be more firmly attached, or more sincerely devoted to England than I am; but when I see importance attached to accusations as ridiculous as they are false, I perceive the liability I am exposed to, to have my tranquillity again broken in upon." He wishes to do anything possible to facilitate the inquiry and free himself from absurd suspicion. Within a few days his friend Edward Storr Haswell came to his aid. Haswell went to the prison of La Force and in the presence of police officers secured from the Prussian, Augustus Assig, a confession that he had been induced to make false charges against his friend and benefactor, Roehenstart, by John Schrader. Assig declared also that John Schrader was employed by the British government and its Paris embassy to collect general information, and that Schrader under pledge of secrecy had told Assig that his principal object was to obtain information and proofs towards the furtherance of a divorce between His Royal Highness the Regent and Her Royal Highness the Princess of Wales. The confession that Haswell secured was forwarded to the British embassy, since Roehenstart had learned that "the inquiries were prompted by the British Government."

That the investigation was initiated from London is made certain by the fact that before Haswell appeared on the scene—in fact only four days after Roehenstart first learned of the affair—the French police had sent to the French ambassador in London, the Marquis d'Osmond, a report exonerating Roehenstart. This report, discovered by the late Henrietta Tayler among the Georgian Papers (22,063–5) in the Royal Archives at Windsor,[1] described Schrader's conduct as exemplifying "ridiculous exaggeration and culpable bad faith." The report (in French) does not mention Assig, and bases its opinion on a personal account of Roehenstart's life:

The situation of Mr. Roehenstart has been much cramped by financial losses. His behavior, reserved and discreet, suits his condition: he sees few people, receives few letters. Both French and foreign agents, charged successively with reporting his moves and his contacts, have displayed, competitively, a zeal surpassing indiscretion when they exaggerate the pretensions of Mr. Roehenstart, who makes not the least pretension and has learned only with the greatest astonishment of the political importance that has been ascribed to him. . . . Nothing in his appearance or in his conversation indicates a man busy with political projects, or one proud of his honorable birth. Humble and submissive, he seemed searching for consolation because of the wretchedness of his position. It is inferred from his explanations about his birth that the marriage of his father and mother took place secretly at Paris without the consent of the Stuart family, who would not have consented to it because of the inferior rank of Monsieur Roehenstart; but after the birth of young Roehenstart, his maternal grandfather recognized the marriage of his daughter and gave an authentic adhesion.

To the inquiries of French police, Roehenstart gave the following account of his life:

I was born at Rome (whither Charles Edward Stuart, Pretender to the throne of England had retired) of the marriage of Charlotte, Duchess of Albany, his daughter, with Auguste Maximilien Roehenstart, the 14th July 1784. After the death of my mother in 1789, my father withdrew to Germany (Munich) where he passed some years and then came to live in London, to which place I accompanied him. He died in 1799. It may be remarked that my father, during much of the time he spent in England, lived in Edinburgh, where also lived the family of the Countess of Albestroff, my maternal grandmother, and it is thus that the place of my birth on my passport is indicated as that city. About two years after the death of my father, I left England to go to Russia, where the Duke and Duchess Alexander de Wurtemberg, uncle and aunt of the emperor, added me to their household as Chamberlain. In 1810 I was obliged to go to London because of interests damaged by the failure of the banker Forbes, to whom all my fortune was entrusted. This same circumstance led me to go to America in the hope of finding this banker, who in fact had

[1] Printed in the *Miscellany* of the Scottish History Society (1951), pp. 132–35.

fled there, and he gave me back a small part of my money. After some years of travel in the New World I came back to London, from where I went to Edinburgh. Desirous of seeing France again, I came here the 25th February last, as my passport shows.

Before leaving England my finances, made painful by the failure just mentioned, forced me to present to the English Government a memoire tending to establish and prove my rights to the succession of the Cardinal Duke of York, my maternal great-uncle. In case the British Government could not see its way to accept this claim, I contracted my pretensions to a pension or to an honorable place, of which I have great need in order to live, not even now being able to support myself except through advances that Mr. Coutts, banker in London, as well as two other friends kindly make me. I had on the subject of this memoire several interviews with Lord Sidmouth which did not destroy my hopes of it.

I must take this occasion to protest against any other project or pretension that could be attributed to me with the intention of doing me harm, and I declare that my views have never passed the bounds of reason and of the duties of an English citizen [*citoyen Anglais*] more jealous of the tranquility of his country than of his own personal happiness, I have never taken any title, or formed any project or undertaken any relationship contrary to these sentiments. I must here make known my true intentions in order to destroy, if possible, the false impressions, that lying reports, with which I have been threatened, may have been able to make concerning me. In this matter I believe I have to fear the villainy of two individuals whose ingratitude and bad faith to me have been evident: the one named Schrader, who himself has told me he served concurrently the French and the English police, and the other, Assig, a Prussian against whom I had to bring charges when he was arrested by the Prefecture of Police for theft.

As to my projects elsewhere, I declare that having the hope that S.M.C. the Emperor of Russia might deign to recommend my claims to the British Government, I will submit to live in whatever place assigned me in order to enjoy in peace the means of livelihood that he will assure me and which I shall regard as a kindness. If this fails, I shall make use of the talents remaining to me by going to take again my employment with S.A.R. the Duke of Wurtemberg in Russia, or make use of my abilities in this country or in Italy. I will give to S.E. the Minister of Police all further information of which he may have need concerning me, and I will make any communications desired; and I have signed this declaration as being the statement of the truth.

(Signed) Edward Roehenstart

This episode is surprising in that, having paid apparently little attention to his naïve Memorial, the British government should go to the length of putting agents on Roehenstart's trail. We do not know why

Roehenstart abbreviated his study of medicine in Edinburgh, and passing through London, went on to Paris. It is a warrantable assumption that he thought the life of a chamberlain might be preferable to that of a physician. We do not know if in passing through London he had "several interviews with Lord Sidmouth," but one doubts it. His hope of a place in Russia was perhaps frustrated by his proud unwillingness to return like a beggar with hat in hand, but he evidently had vain hopes of a return. How he and Haswell became involved with a type like Assig is problematical, but travelers make strange contacts, and Assig had had, according to Haswell, some "rank in society."

The episode closed, Roehenstart was on the wing for Germany, where he was possibly in company with a lady whom later he sometimes calls his aunt and sometimes "the Countess." She is unnamed (and at this time even unmentioned) but in 1833 she will somewhat emerge in the story. We learn of this 1817 journey in two letters from Roehenstart to a typical friend, named Daniel Ellis, who is making the grand tour, and is ready to leave Switzerland and move on to Italy—possibly with the hope of meeting Roehenstart there. Roehenstart had hoped to go to Russia, but he now informs Ellis: "I have received unsatisfactory news from Russia, and will postpone my going to Petersburg. I think seriously of setting out in the course of three weeks for Naples, where I will remain untill some happy change takes place in my affairs." Later in July, Roehenstart has changed plans: he must first go to Wiesbaden, but still hopes to see Ellis in Naples. It is possible that this is the first journey to be mentioned on which he escorts his unnamed aunt to Naples, a type of travel that later appears frequently.

Perhaps the two men met in Naples, but a letter of January 3, 1818, indicates that because Naples proved to be expensive, or for some other reason, Roehenstart spent a part of the winter in Genoa. His letters indicate a considerable resentment against the British government for putting spies on his conduct and for the government's harshness in dealing with humble rioters in the north of England. Charlotte, Princess of Wales, the only probable successor to her father, then King George IV, had died in November, and on that event Roehenstart comments to Ellis:

Most sincerely do I deplore the Princess's untimely death: it is certainly a great national calamity. I can say with truth that from some reasons I was acquainted with, I almost knew that this shocking event would take place. Soon after the unhappy marriage, I mentioned to some friends that I was confident that Pr's Charlotte either could not realize the hope of the Nation in having an heir, or that her pregnancy should be attended with great danger for her life. I bitterly regret to see my omen justified by the event.

The death of the one hopeful heir to the throne and the severe repression by Lord Sidmouth of riots in Derby and elsewhere were causes of a national melancholy. Spies and informers had been employed against others as well as against Roehenstart. There must have glimmered in the back of other minds than his own vague nostalgic recollections of 1715 and 1745. None of the surviving seven sons of George III had in 1817 any legitimate offspring: the Princess Victoria was not yet born.

CHAPTER EIGHT

Early Aftermath

Roehenstart before 1816—perhaps even before going to Russia—habitually had lived a wandering life. After 1816 this love of travel operated increasingly. For a while there were almost annual journeys from Dresden or Baden to Italy—most frequently to Naples. There were also the longer journeys, one to America and several to the Levant. By preference he liked to live in Italy, but he also spent a considerable amount of time in Paris. During most of 1819 he was the paid cicerone of two young gentlemen, named Dirck and Alewyn, who wished to "do" the Levant. This voyage ended disastrously if one may believe a long letter that Roehenstart sent to his *chère grand maman*, the Countess of Albany, early in 1820. The voyage had not been so profitable financially as Roehenstart had hoped, but by the same "cruel fatality which has not ceased to afflict our family" he was shipwrecked on his return in Mount's Bay. A part of his letter demands quotation:

> I had the bad luck to be shipwrecked in the month of December last on the coast of Cornwall, in Mount's Bay. All my possessions were the booty of the waves, and I owe my life to Providence, which in this great danger gave me sufficient presence of mind to save myself by swimming. I shall add with satisfaction that I had the good fortune to save two of my companions in disaster. Having got ashore, exhausted from fatigue and cold, I was forced to undergo a long quarantine, because my ship came from Smyrna, and the excessive expenses have entirely used up the small resources remaining to me. But I ought not to fatigue you, my dear mother, with details of my debts: they are, alas, in a truly bad way.

One has to suspect his story for reasons perhaps trivial. He had saved himself and two companions, but no possessions. But preserved among his papers there is an account book for the voyage with day by day listings from February 15 to October 1, 1819, of every smallest expense—and the book shows no sign of ever having been wet. Possibly he drew it up during his tedious quarantine, but it purports to be a day-by-day record made in the various spots where money was disbursed by himself or his two charges. He came ashore, he says, with no possessions; but he complains bitterly of the treatment received from customs officers—who would hardly be levying duties on properties at the bottom of Mount's Bay. It is quite possible that the shipwreck was invented to arouse pity and secure a loan from his *chère grand maman.* He carried his protests against the customs officers straight to headquarters, and Lord Chetwynd promised to investigate the officers at Marazion. An unidentified friend, H. F. Nashe, in August wrote to Roehenstart about the death of a "mutual friend," who may have been a fellow voyager. Nashe is not inclined to suspect the physician of causing the death, but he is suspicious as to the disappearance of a letter of credit—which must have come ashore by swimming!

Another passage in this "shipwreck" letter, less picturesque but more vital announces Roehenstart's marriage:

> It is, however, my duty finally to break this cruel silence in order to inform you of my marriage with an Italian lady, brought up in Paris, of the Barbuonei[1] family. This house, though not rich, is distinguished and is of a rather ancient nobility. My wife is forever speaking to me of the pleasure she would feel in having the honor of being presented to you. . . . I am sure she would study to win your favor.

This passage is the only mention of his first wife preserved in these papers, except for the original of a certificate showing that on July 20, 1821, Maria Antoinetta Sophia Countess of Roehenstart, aged thirty-one, was buried in the Parish of St. Mary-le-Bone, in the County of Middlesex. One is inclined to suppose that Roehenstart left Naples in the winter of 1817–18 for Genoa because of his interest in this lady, whom he at about that time married. For the year 1818 there is almost a total lack of papers in his collection, and one trusts that this fact indicates that the young couple were too happy to bother about keeping records of their happiness. During 1819, when voyaging in the Levant he kept no copies of letters that he might have written to his wife. In 1821 within a week after his countess was buried he started posthaste on a journey to Turin or Milan, evidently to take the news of the death,

[1] The name is illegibly written, and is here guessed at.

and settle some financial matters attendant upon it. He was back in England in a fortnight.

The letter announcing this marriage was sent to the Countess of Albany, possibly his only recognized relative. When in 1824 she in turn died, the obituary notices gave Roehenstart some reason to insist that she was the *second* wife of Prince Charles, the first having been his grandmother the Countess of Albestroff. As he ceased to have hopes of favors from George IV, Roehenstart was increasingly watchful of mentions of the Jacobite Stuarts in the public press. As early as 1816 when John Stanier Clarke's *Life of James II* appeared, with a statement that it was based "on the Stuart Papers at Carlton House," Roehenstart wrote, and perhaps somewhere published, an adverse comment in which he insisted, with no justification, that the papers at Carlton House (which had been purchased from Abbé Waters, the major domo of Charlotte Stuart) were unauthentic, since the original papers and manuscripts had been removed and secured before Mr. de l'Eau (as he calls Waters) had any access to the library in Florence. The passage is typical of Roehenstart's methods of rewriting history to fit his purposes. Among his papers there is an account, not written by him, but sent to him from Rome, of the purchase of the second (Rome) lot of Stuart papers, as managed in part by Dr. Robert Watson. His longest historical effort, written to "correct" the obituary of the Countess of Albany, was printed in the *New Times*, March 18, 1824.

Either the editor, Sir John Stoddart, or a subordinate, corrupted one of Roehenstart's sentences to read, "Prince Charles Edward . . . was first married to the Princess of Stolberg." This mistake called forth immediate protest from one of Roehenstart's friends. Roehenstart never signed his name to any of these contributions. His story in the *New Times* was signed "A Friend to Unfortunate Princes." In this article he gives the following account of himself, without giving his own name. He says the Duchess of Albany

> . . . had married a Nobleman, descending in a direct line from the Earl of Darnley, husband of Mary, Queen of Scotland: his being a Protestant was the reason for keeping their marriage secret; the Dutchess was afraid of irritating her father; but when she had a son, the marriage could be no longer concealed: she obtained her father's pardon, and Prince Charles Edward gave his name to his grandson.
>
> This Representative of the Stuarts, whom I perfectly know, has been the sport of that cruel Fortune which weighed with an iron hand upon his family, and though still in the prime of life, has, for the last twelve years, met with

such a variety of complicated misfortunes, that if related, they would appear almost incredible.—In poverty and seclusion he supports his situation with a fortitude worthy of a better fate.

One had best regard much of what Roehenstart says about the "last" Stuarts as "almost incredible." He ennobles the Walkinshaws, makes Charlotte Stuart born in wedlock, and here has possibly invented a new father for himself, descended from Darnley—though later he decided that his ancestor was not Darnley but Darnley's uncle James Moray Stuart.

His attitude towards the Countess of Albany had grown more hostile as time went on. At first she had seemed helpful, and one wonders if briefly she had shown flirtatious feelings towards Roehenstart. In some quarters raised eyebrows were seen. As late as 1839, when the Countess was long dead, there was gossip, and Roehenstart commented to Mrs. Hamilton of Kames Castle on "appalling rumors":

Have you by any chance discovered who is the Lady who communicated that appalling intelligence respecting me? It is so preposterously absurd that I feel no one who knows me can for a moment entertain a shadow of a doubt of its falsehood.—My step grandmother was certainly a very bad woman, a disgrace to our name, but notwithstanding the numerous proofs of her hatred towards me, I could scarcely have believed her capable of aspersions of this nature.

There was genuine friendliness on neither side of the relationship between Roehenstart and his *chère grand maman.*

It will be recalled that Roehenstart's first wife died in 1821. At the end of 1826 he married a second time. The lady was Louisa Constance, daughter of the late Bouchier Smith, Esq. The father had been a close friend of the Earl of Coventry; he had apparently died in Coventry House in 1822. Constance was probably a cousin of Mrs. Fitzherbert, "wife of George IV." Roehenstart may have been introduced to Mrs. Smith and her daughter by Count Gabriel de Sampigny, whom Roehenstart had met in America, and whose path several times crossed that of Roehenstart. Sampigny wrote to Roehenstart on September 15, 1823, about the Smiths:

Mrs. Bouchier Smith is the lady to whom you had the kindness to bring a letter for me last year, she has become a widow and thinks to settle in France. I am excessively fond of her although we haven't seen each other for more than 25 years, and I am well requited, which is a proof that we both are *lovers by nature.*

The lady, as Sampigny also wrote, pressingly invited him to come to England for a visit to her and her daughter; but when this was written Roehenstart already knew that there were legal difficulties (involving a large sum of money) looming between the Smiths (or Smythes) and the Sampignys. It was alleged and denied that a lady of the Sampigny family had paid a considerable sum of money to a Mr. Walther Smythe, which it was desired to recover. The Smith story was that the money had never been received. Out of this disagreeable situation (or some other) there arose a strong animosity on the part of Roehenstart towards his former friend.

Roehenstart's courtship need not have been hasty, but the marriage, which took place at St. Pancras's on December 13, 1826, may well have been almost an elopement. One suspects that someone, very likely Sampigny, had prejudiced the mother against the match. At any rate a few days after the ceremony, Mrs. Stuart (as Roehenstart's second wife called herself) wrote from Richmond a heartbroken letter begging for her mother's forgiveness—and a reconciliation. There was a suspicion that Roehenstart had financial advantage in mind in this match, and Constance takes pains to reassure her mother on this point:

Let me take this opportunity of saying that my Annuity is so secured that were it possible for affairs to turn ever so badly, *you* my dearest Mama would ever have a right to partake of it, let this assurance calm your mind upon the future, and ever believe me your truly affectionate Daughter.
Direct to Mrs. Stuart
Post Office
Richmond

Mrs. Stuart, though unaware of it, had already learned one thing about her mobile husband: the address normally would be poste restante. Apart from bits of summarized fragments of letters sent to his wife by Roehenstart she hardly gets mentioned in his papers. In the early thirties Mrs. Stuart lived for a time at Abbéville, was much in Paris, but did not go from there to Italy with her husband on his many journeys to that country. She complained of being left alone, and Roehenstart countered with assurances that the aunt whom he escorted to Naples was disagreeable, and that he was far from leading a gay life, as Mrs. Stuart suspected. The aunt was perhaps financially interesting.

In the winter of 1828/29 the couple had a house at Andernach near Neuwied, and a letter to an unnamed colonel, who is spoken of as one whose family had been loyal supporters of Prince Charles Edward, invited him to join Roehenstart and his wife as guest for the winter. The letter gives a picture of something more like home life than we get elsewhere. Roehenstart writes:

> At Neuwied—If you have not yet settled upon a place of residence for the winter, and if you condescend to accept an apartment in the better part of a house which I have rented for six months at Ehrenbreitstein, my wife and I shall think ourselves extremely happy to have the honour to receive you. We live much retired and know how to pass our time in an agreeable manner free from the need of running after the pleasures of society. Your rooms separate from ours will leave you at liberty to join us only at the hour of dinner, or if you even prefer, I will have you served by yourself. A little music, some good books, whist, chess, &c will make us pass the long winter evenings—I can also furnish you with authoritative information concerning the Turks, whom I know perfectly well:—but I perceive that I look like a merchant trying to sell his wares. My only wish is to see you accept.

At this time and later we get only scattered glimpses of Roehenstart's life. In 1831 he and Mrs. Stuart were back in London for a part of the year—possibly in connection with a suit in chancery. The torn top part of a letter, in the handwriting of Sampigny, is addressed to Messieurs Fladgate, No. 13 Essex Street, London. At the top of the remaining slip of paper is written "Mrs. Smith / 38 North Audeley Street" and the fragment of the letter (written in French) says:

> Such is the name of the people of this business who have conferred with Mr. Walther Smythe who has confessed before them to have made the agreement in question. These gentlemen know the address in the city and in the country of M. Walther Smythe, brother of Mme Fitzheiberg [Fitzherbert?].

A different suit in chancery concerning property left by Mrs. Stuart's father, Mr. Bouchier Smith, was about this time apparently successfully defended; for at Abbéville in December Mrs. Stuart received a chancery order for slightly over £67.

During the early thirties Roehenstart was for long periods away from his wife. In 1832 and 1833, if not for a longer time, he was attached to H.M.S. "St. Vincent" (120 guns, the largest man-of-war in the eastern Mediterranean at this time) as courier or perhaps as interpreter or instructor in languages. His name is not in the *Navy Lists* of officers assigned to the "St. Vincent," but he writes as if he were such, and so he seems to have been treated. At any rate he had some sort of very pleasant arrangement, which during the summer months enabled him to tour the Levant. In August, 1833, Mrs. Stuart followed the ship to Malta, and there awaited her husband. His interesting adventures in the Levant—archeological and social—represent perhaps his happiest days. He loved to study ancient Greek remains and enjoyed observing the manners of men wherever he went.

During the winter months he was less pleasantly employed in squiring his unidentified "aunt," a countess, back and forth from Germany to Naples. Such services to this somewhat arrogant faded beauty (as he describes her) are to be explained doubtless as a means of increasing his income. Our knowledge of his naval activities comes from extensive travel diaries or letters; knowledge of his movements when ashore comes either from the brief summaries that he kept of letters to Mrs. Stuart or from much-visaed passports that show his journeys about Italy and occasionally into Germany.

A British passport issued at Paris on April 22, 1835, has especial interest as giving in the unimaginative tabular manner of passports a description of Roehenstart's physical appearance in middle age:

Age	48 years [b. 1787?]
Height	1 m. 70 c. [5 feet 7 inches]
Hair	gray
Forehead	[word illegible from creasing in the paper]
Eyebrows	gray
Eyes	blue
Nose	niogre[?]
Mouth	m^{e} [moyenne?]
Chin	round
Face	oval
Complexion	coloré [ruddy?]
Signes particulières	none

This passport was used chiefly in trips from Germany to Naples. The identity of the "aunt" whom he accompanied is uncertain. One thinks of some lady from the Rohan family who lived in Germany. Charlotte, Princess of Rohan, was actually Roehenstart's aunt. She lived at times in or near Baden, a region that Roehenstart seems to have frequented. But other possibilities such as a sister of the Countess of Albany (Louise von Stolberg) must be considered. Certainly if he called Louise "maman," he might call her sister "aunt." On one occasion by her orders heavy pieces of furniture, against Roehenstart's advice, were brought from Florence (where the Countess of Albany had lived) to

Germany. Of the aunt Roehenstart writes to his wife: "she has a bad heart and is the counterpart of the C. of Albany." No certain conclusion as to her identity has been reached.

Roehenstart may have disliked his aunt as much as he tells his wife that he did, but he greatly liked Naples, as the bits from the letters written to his wife indicate. He particularly liked the region about Castellamare which in his jotted notes he calls a "delightful spot, classical recollections & learning returning by degree into my thick head—I walk the silent streets." An animated description of Pompeii—"went to see the eruption which they call mine & the horse fell, the rein broke & I jumped out and rolled in the dust with a slight contusion & very narrow escape—the horse was killed on the spot having two legs broken and the poor man died the following morning!" Roehenstart flattered himself on his knowledge of volcanoes—and he was in several traffic accidents. The episode is typical.

After the thirties, from which come his episodes about Naples, we have, apart from his travel diaries in the Levant, few papers and little information about Roehenstart. In August, 1836, he sent his wife a copy of a piece designed for the *Glasgow Chronicle* with a very friendly letter addressed to "Madame Stuart, rue du Harley No. 4 au Marais, Paris." That constitutes the latest mention of Mrs. Stuart in these papers. One judges that she predeceased her husband and left no children: there is no known date for her death.

If we turn from Roehenstart's family environment to that of his commonly mentioned friends, we find our attention focused on Paris and Baden or the Rhine Valley. There is no doubt that he had considerable gifts for making friendships readily. At times to be sure, like an Ancient Mariner he must needs hold the new acquaintance with a glittering tale of his "reclamations." Normally he found willing listeners. His manner of life, being migratory, led him to have many apparently temporary friends, chiefly among English or Russian travelers making the grand tour. His passion for giving information led him to write letters to many such acquaintances. He was well informed in divers fields. He writes with some interest of volcanoes, iron bridges, and of "wild poetic Scotland" as well as of literary subjects. Many of these letters come to our knowledge only in replies from friends who compliment him on his charm as a writer of letters.

There is also a less pleasant side of his gifts for friendship. He could become enraged with a friend and write extremely abusive letters in his rages. A sort of suspicion of others' scorn existed but did not dominate in Roehenstart's friendships; but there are two cases which show a ready rage that suggest its existence. The first case is that of Messence, Count de la Garde, whose *Voyage* (1824) caused a violent rupture of his friendship with Roehenstart. They were uneasy friends in London, where at the time the book was published Messence remained, while Roehenstart went to Paris, attended to the reading of proofs, and other aspects of publication, including the writing of reviews. Either these services or a partial collaboration in the writing induced Roehenstart to claim an equal part in the book with Messence. Lack of recognition of this fact or some unknown cause led Roehenstart to break with Messence and to write to him intolerably abusive letters. He began by calling Messence a liar, continued with the avowed convication "that you are entirely incapable of writing alone the least thing. You have without doubt some wit, some facility with a couplet, but that's all." Messence was told that his awkwardness in society made him the laughing stock of all polite people; that his title as count was falsely assumed, and Roehenstart ends a second letter with a climax to his accusations, as follows:

> . . . all these things are of little importance for you, and I knew them already myself; but what inspired me with profound horror is that it is alleged [in a secret report of the police on Messence] *that you were arrested and imprisoned in Italy for stealing jewels*!

And so shortly after the publication of the *Voyage* this friendship ended. One doubts if many of Roehenstart's accusations had other grounds than his own extreme rage.

A similar and less justifiable break occurred with the Count de Sampigny not later than 1828. There had been earlier disenchantments in this friendship, which began in America. The troubles were chiefly over money matters. Roehenstart always insisted that Sampigny had exacted double payment of an American loan, and it is clear that Roehenstart was never prompt in repaying loans from Sampigny. From 1816 to 1824, and perhaps longer, they were reconciled friends, and Sampigny did a number of kindly services for Roehenstart. There were troubles other than money probably. Fundamentally Sampigny seems to have been slightly amused at times by Roehenstart's "reclamations." He was effusive in protestations of friendship, but he writes facetiously of Roehenstart's coming glory, calls him "my sovereign," and gets off quips about Roehenstart's marrying a rich princess when probably he knows that Roehenstart is going to marry a girl named Smith. He was very ready to make small loans, but his notion of good manners did not prevent repeated requests for repayment.

He introduced Roehenstart to distinguished elderly friends, who, he thought, might be of considerable service to Roehenstart. Two of these Nestors were probably General Lenormand de Bretteville and a M. Cales (unidentified: the name is badly written). They did not at once justify Sampigny's hopes for his friend's advancement. We shall hear more of the General. Two other gentlemen may have made Roehenstart's acquaintance through Sampigny. One signs himself D'Entraigues, and evidently thinks Roehenstart might have influence in getting an unnamed person a promotion or a decoration in the French army. D'Entraigues writes from the Château de Montgioroux near Sezanne, and hopes when in Paris "to continue that gentlemanly intercourse which has already been so interesting and agreeable." The other, the Comte D'Angles, a French minister, privy councilor, and industrialist, got Roehenstart interested in investing in a factory for manufacturing steam engines or in an iron forge. Roehenstart got his friend B. Beale a position with the company, and eventually both of them lost money in the affair. Roehenstart avows that he is through with speculations.

The matter that finally separated him from Sampigny was probably an unpleasant affair with a rascal named Herculès. He was apparently a cardsharper who had the misfortune to cheat Roehenstart out of a sum, probably Fr. 500. Roehenstart detecting the cheat undertook to expose the man in the law courts. Sampigny thought that if Roehenstart could afford to go to law, he could afford to pay him the Fr. 175 (plus interest) owing to him. He evidently reported the Herculès affair to Constance Smith's mother, and so seemed to try to prevent Roehenstart's marriage. In 1828 Roehenstart decided to pay Sampigny, and sent a most abusive letter to him by the hand of a common friend, the Comte de Soyecourt. The Count, however, refused to intervene and urged Roehenstart to calm his rage and be reconciled to Sampigny. The year 1828, however, apparently saw the end of the relationship—which had involved estrangement at least two years earlier.

From such unpleasantness we may turn to the friendship with General de Bretteville, who was, after the death of the Prince de Limbourg, the active head of the Ordre d'Ancienne Noblesse et des 4 Empereurs d'Allemagne. In 1822, eager to revive the order, which had fallen into decay as result of the Revolution, the General wished to employ Roehenstart in finding a new Grand Maître—who had to be a ruling sovereign. This order had been conferred on Roehenstart, it will be remembered, by the king of France in 1818. When in 1822 Sampigny went to visit the General at Montgeron, he carried the information that Roehenstart felt he must have a more official, documented commission for the task of finding a Grand Maître. He got an official letter of appointment as *interprète* of the wishes of the order to obtain the consent of a sovereign prince to become Grand Maître. It seems doubtful if he had any success with the reigning princes. He offered the post to Ernest, reigning Duke of Saxe-Coburg, who, if he replied at all to the offer, did not reply without prodding. The post was also offered to the Prince Royal of Bavaria, with results unknown. The awkwardness of awaiting a reply from Duke Ernest of Saxe-Coburg led to some correspondence with the Duke's younger brother, Prince Leopold, whom Roehenstart had known slightly in earlier years. On the whole it is doubtful if activities for this order won any notable prestige for Roehenstart, but it occupied him much in 1822–25, and it does represent him in somewhat higher circles than elsewhere.

His friendships span a large segment of society. At the top they include the Duke of Württemberg in Russia, the Duke of Gloucester, a royal cousin in England, and Prince Joseph von Hohenlohe, a friend and "fellow officer." Lower down his friends include, as his letters show, various travelers, and at least one true rascal. To be sure the rascal bore the distinguished name of Herculès, and called himself both baron and marquis. Most of Roehenstart's friends lie in between these extremes: friendly travelers have left most traces in Roehenstart's papers, but he seems to have had firm and permanent friends in London and Paris and possibly in Munich and other cities. Most of these relationships can be followed only vaguely, for they are normally both obscure and tantalizing. For us much of Roehenstart's social life must somewhat resemble a masked ball. The following note, for example, undated and unplaced and possibly written in a disguised hand in French, might come from any period in his life and from any capital city whether St. Petersburg, Paris, Vienna, or any other:

> One desires most strongly to see and talk with you. You are consequently begged to be this evening at the ball at the opera. A blue ribbon and the name of Margueritte, to which you will answer, will show whether you have been so kind as to grant this entreaty. It will be a keen affliction but no surprise not to see you. The manner of this request doubtless gives a reason for refusing it, but perhaps you will see that this is the only means of arranging it, and that

this occasion once lost might not be recovered; the matter which one wishes to confide to you requires as much speed as discretion. May this hope not be in vain!

At half past one the bench in the middle of the foyer opposite the door.
Monday morning

CHAPTER NINE

Travels

Travel, one may safely say, was Roehenstart's favorite occupation. As early as 1814 he applied for a British passport, and then, and probably before then, he chose to regard himself as English. His fictitious father was said to have been born in England in 1740, and the son is forever speaking of his countrymen or his fair countrywomen, meaning English men or women. He told the French police in 1817 that he and his father had lived before 1800 in London and Edinburgh, and he had a passport giving Edinburgh (wrongly, he confessed) as his birthplace. No national roots gave him a settled place of residence in England or Scotland, and he spent much of his time in travel, chiefly on the Continent or in the Levant. A youthful experience as a soldier fighting the Turks may possibly account for a continuing interest in the Levant. In a letter to Mrs. Hamilton (1839) he speaks of leaving the army in disgust after Austerlitz and of his hasty exit from Russia, and he continues: "I have since traveled much, visited every quarter of the globe, & made the regular voyage round the world." Mrs. Hamilton was not the only person to whom this much-wandering was detailed. The Barone di Carnea of Vienna wrote of Roehenstart as a pleasant acquaintance, "un uomo stimabile il quale avea veduto il Ganges ed il Mississippi." One may indeed doubt—though one cannot be certain—if Roehenstart ever saw either river: the romance of travel traditionally has a connection with romancing. The loving Indian princess whom he says he left behind him in America is doubtless pure fiction. Possibly he speaks truth of an experienced thrill when he writes of the happiness felt when "vaulting on my noble arabian I bounded over the desert." Greece and Turkey he certainly visited more than once. Other regions —even Iceland or French West Africa and the Niger—he talks of. He very likely visited Spain more than once, but the only sure visit to that country is one made in the last year of his life. Of Russia and Sweden his papers say practically nothing after 1811.

We know certainly that he went from Russia to England and America in 1811–12; we know that after 1814 he was frequently back and forth from south Germany to Naples and other Italian cities. He has left us accounts of much that he saw in Italy and Switzerland in 1814–16. One judges that Baden and Bavaria as well as France were so well known that he felt no urge to record his life in those regions. In 1818–19 he was traveling with two young men, Alewyn and Dirck, from Amsterdam to Naples and Messina, and from there through Greece and Asia Minor. In the early thirties in his undefined capacity as aide to the admiral (Sir Charles Hotham) on board H.M.S. "St. Vincent," he visited Lisbon, and made extensive visits to Athens, Constantinople, Smyrna, the plains of Troy, and several of the Aegean Islands.

Of these voyages in the Levant Roehenstart has left fragmentary but interesting manuscript accounts, which, as they exist in the form of journals, were written casually and revised intermittently and imperfectly. These journals he made from letters to various friends, especially to members of a family in England named Brunnurn (the name is variously spelled by Roehenstart). Other letters to unnamed persons are also related to his journals. His travel-writing thus varies from the informal epistolary or journalistic manner to the style of a factual guide book. There are even some imaginative travel fantasies, sufficiently glowing to be at once placed as such.

The height of fantasy seems to exist in his French *Fragment d'un voyage sentimental*, which in letters from "Rochester" to "Eulalie" (*vertueuse épouse d'Edouard*) tell of his voyage from Naples to Egypt and Turkey. Rochester seems to be a courier carrying documents to ambassadors—an employment that suggests Roehenstart's possible function in the thirties. A friendship with Volezzo, nephew of Cardinal Quirini, does not suggest Roehenstart. In Alexandria, Rochester is befriended by the banker Hollpensonk, who, after the traveler has visited the pyramids and other antiquities, treats him as a son. Rochester suddenly turns painter, and does a charming portrait of the ravishingly beautiful Androsine, young daughter of Hollpensonk. But the ship is ordered to carry dispatches to Constantinople, and more melancholy than ever, Rochester must leave these new friends. In Constantinople the enormously wealthy Turk Zagaa-Bassa takes over the function of patron for Rochester:

He has offered me garments of cloth of gold: he has given me three Ethiopian women to make my tea in the morning; he has added to them ten African slaves; three to serve me sherbet; three to arrange my sopha; and the four last to await my orders. That is not all: I have three young white women subjected to my rule: one brings me perfumes; the others accompany me to the baths.

So in part runs this oriental apologue, and yet (we are told), without Eulalie, all this is simply ground for added melancholy—and so the fragment ends. It is far too much aglow with the sentimentality of Sterne. It may have some basis in Roehenstart's own voyage to Egypt, but Rochester is represented as a painter, whereas Roehenstart, a moderately good maker of sketches and maps, made no pretense to the use of the brush. The real traveler and Rochester have only their sentimentality in common.

The account of his voyage with Alewyn and Dirck is quite another matter. Here Roehenstart is the cicerone: his notes are those of a guide-book—and doubtless most of them are compilations from printed sources. In one manuscript he details the daily expenses of the voyage for all three men, and in another he gives a mass of factual detail concerning geography, topography, history, government, and major edifices—and anecdotes, usually interesting. It will be remembered that when he crossed the Atlantic, he carried with him several volumes about America, and in preparation for his voyage of 1818–19 he gave Alewyn a list of books that the young man should provide for the occasion. The list reads:

Notes of the books that I believe necessary at this time
for M. Alewyn:

Le Cours complet des mathematiques de l'Ecole Polytechnique
L'Histoire ancienne de Rollin
Continuation de la même par Crévier
Vies des hommes illustres de Plutarque
Abrégé des histoires Greque et Romaine par Dr. [Oliver] Goldsmith

For modern history and geography:
Histoire de l'Europe moderne et etat de l'Europe par Campbell
[i.e. John Campbell's *Political State of Europe* (1750?)]
Histoire de Charles V par Robertson
[1] Essai sur les provinces unies par Sir W. Temple
Le siècle de Louis XIV par Voltaire

[2] Histoire d'Angleterre [3] Histoire de France*
Grammaire historique et gèographique de Guthrie

For the English, French, Italian, and German languages I have several elementary books; so it is useless to buy others.
Le Cours de littérature francaise is enough for the moment.
The Spectator and the works of Pope
Gerusalemme liberata
Works of Schiller

I assume that Mr. A. already has the greater part of the Greek and Latin authors.

For moral philosophy:
Locke's Essay on the Human Understanding
Burke's Inquiry into the Sublime and Beautiful
Elements of the Philosophy of the Human Mind by Dugald Stuart

With Roehenstart as governor, young Mr. Alewyn was in for no merely gay and fashionable cruise: the voyage was designed as an educational experience. It is notable that this list of books includes no works on eastern antiquities. Those were furnished by Roehenstart himself, who at Ephesus cites, for example, Pocock, Chandler, and Dallaway. On extensive voyages Roehenstart went armed with books on the regions to be visited. On a later voyage, when the "St. Vincent" was anchored near Smyrna, he conducted visitors over the ship and, if he liked them and if they knew the French language, showed them "my little cabin and my books." There was escapism in Roehenstart's fondness for travel, but there was more than that: he had a real and intellectual curiosity about the history and nature of civilization, and he loved to instruct others.

With Alewyn and Dirck he spent the first week of June, 1819, in Sicily and then sailed away to Zante and other Greek islands, to Patras Corinth, and above all to Athens. Roehenstart's prepared notes (lecture notes?) on Athens—its history, topography, classical remains together with illustrations of Greek manners—run to about fifty large quarto pages, and must have been most informational to his protégés. From Athens they made less extensive visits to Smyrna, Ephesus, Constantinople, the more historic Aegean Islands, and to Jerusalem, Bethlehem, and the Dead Sea. At the end of the year they returned to England, and allegedly suffered shipwreck in Mount's Bay. The final

* The function of the three superscript digits is obscure.

financial settlements for this voyage were difficult and, for Roehenstart, unsatisfactory. His notes contain little narrative of the voyage: they consist chiefly of information, assembled from books for the use of the two young men for whom he was cicerone.

Far more personal are the results of his observations made chiefly in the year 1833 during the period when he was attached to H.M.S. "St. Vincent." In 1832 the ship was stationed for a time at Lisbon, and in eight folio pages he writes up the current struggle between Don Miguel and Don Pedro for the Portuguese throne: this again is an educational project addressed to "my dear Dorcas"—who is unidentified. Late in June, 1833, begin the journals, which as letters to the Brunnurn family, recount his more significant travels in the Levant. He records fully his experiences at Constantinople, where he spent a month at this time. The rest of his journal concerns chiefly the plain of Troy, the site of which he studied during some days, Smyrna, where Turkish hospitality is attractively described, and the islands of Delos and Pharos, among others. A separate manuscript, somewhat in the manner of a guidebook, gives an account of Egypt as visited by Roehenstart and his fellow officers.

Among the Turks Roehenstart ceases to be the collector of essential details from other travelers, and sets down his own interests and impressions. His taste for antiquities had been early heightened by reading Humboldt and by visits to Herculaneum and Pompeii. From visits to Vesuvius he contracted a keen interest in volcanoes. He prophesied the time of an eruption, and prided himself on his awareness of the habits of volcanoes. He visited Mt. Etna, and, characteristically, was in on one of the more spectacular volcanic events of his time, the submarine eruption that created Graham's Island. On a day in July, when his ship was at anchor in the harbor of Valetta (Malta), Roehenstart heard the report of John Cannino that he had seen the sea on fire near Sicily. This report was laughed at, but "the arrival the same afternoon of some small vessels soon confirmed the Signor Cannino's report." About a fortnight thereafter Roehenstart visited the new island and in his notes gives a detailed description of it. Where Roehenstart is something exciting is likely to emerge—though only once in a lifetime is it a newborn island.

His interest in the Levant, which possibly dates from his early military career, was confirmed by his reading and by an eager curiosity about the mores of strange lands, and by his sympathy with the Greek struggle for freedom from the Turks. It led naturally to an interest in classical antiquities. Athens he viewed with careful veneration—though lamenting the decay and the crudeness of modern Athens. His personal reactions here are studious: he is skeptical as to the knowledge of the local antiquarian, M. Fauvel, but is at times less impressionistic than usual. Witness, for example, his "Memo 2d Sept. 1833" made at the Parthenon:

Diam of the Cols of the Parthenon—measured by myself in the presence of Mon[r] Pettarki on the 2d of Sept. 1833 were as under
Viz—35 Cols are now standing—their diam[s] at the Base
SIX FEET TWO INCHES—and 34 feet in height
Memo 2 Sept. 1833 of the Olympian
16 Cols remain stand—diam—*seven feet* / height *sixty feet*
Measured by myself 2 Sept[r] 1833

A recurring theme is Roehenstart's reprobation of thefts of ancient sculptures, etc., by the English and others. He quotes Lord Byron's comment "scratched on the stone and mortar that replaced what Lord Elgin had carried off": *Quod Gothi non fecerunt Scoti facierent.* A more usual tone is the rhapsody sent in his third letter to Milborne Brunnurn in 1832:

You, my dear Milburn, who are now become a classic, how I envy your acquirement—How often do I think of my dear friends, at Bradwell as I wander among the ruined temples. We have Stuart, Robinson, Dr. Clark, Dodwell, Gill, and Chandler, and Leake with us as our fellow travellers. The Elligant Stuart exclaims in the delight which he experiences on this visit to Athens: "Here reason and voluptousness flowed from the mouth of the virtuous Epicurus! There the ameable Plato inculcated philosophy and virtue! Cruel Sylla to deprive posterity of the sacred groves of the Academy in which Aristotle as he strayed propounded the deepest questions of metaphysics and morality—Yonder was the Areopagus—here stood the Odeum. This entire temple is that of Theseus, it seems to have been built but yesterday—around are the ruins of Minerva, of the Acropolis and the Pantheon. Here the heroism, the science and the arts reached the highest degree of perfection to which the human mind is capable of attaining. These ideas present to the imagination a succession of scenes ever new and ever pleasing; my heart is penetrated with them; it palpitates: a soft melancholy succeeds these ecstasies. I yield to the pleasing illusion, and indulge in my reveries till they at length vanish like "the baseless fabric of a vision."

Freed briefly from the printed authors who are his fellow travelers the "Elligant Stuart" has given us more of a rhapsody than is usual with him. He has a further gift for detailing modern instances of survivals in folklore of classical customs. Such is his account of the continuing use of worship of the goddess Lucina in Athens:

As the moon was also considered a goddess that had the care of childbirth it was under the influence of her light that the youthful brides of Athens with uplifted garments slid down the Lucinian stone, a portion of the red marble rock on which stood the temple dedicated to the goddess, which was thought an infalable token of divine favor. The goddess was thus invoked, by maidens to secure the virtuous affections of their lover, and to hasten a marriage pure and unspotted as Luna's rock, and by those who were with child that they might be delivered without pain. . . . This ceremony still exists, and many an Athenian maid, is at this day detected in stealing out at midnight smoothly and silently to slide down Lucina's rock, whose temple has been succeeded by the Church of the Holy Virgin, who is now invoked instead of the fair goddess of silent hour.

Ancient edifices of Athens surviving in 1833 are described, but here Roehenstart offers little that is new or personal in his comments. Later when the "St. Vincent" is at anchor off the greater Delos, he gives an interesting account of that almost deserted island as he found it on August 21, 1833:

On landing we immediately directed our course to Mount Cynthus, a rocky and insignificant height, the summit of which we reached in twenty minutes. Here we found the foundation of a small temple of white marble with a portion of tesilated pavement. From this you command an extensive view of the Islands. Mount Cynthus must have fallen off wonderfully in size since the days of Dianas hunting, for there is scarcely space and food sufficient for the twenty goats I counted climbing the precipices and seeking a scanty subsistence amid the ruins of the temples whose mossy fragments having rolled from the summit lay scattered around the declining [declivity?] of the mountain. In descending we discovered the remains of a beautiful Theatre constructed of white marble in an excellent state of preservation. Wandering amid the ruins we hit upon the pedestal of the statue of Apollo, an enormous block of white marble 15 feet by 12 and three feet thick. The inscription ΑΠΟΛΛΩΝ is very plainly to be read on the plinth of the pedestal. Our party dined on this stone. The mutilated figure itself lays a few yards as you walk from the beech to the left of the Pedistal. The trunk of the figure alone remains laying with the back upwards, deprived of the head, arms, and the lower part, which terminated in the tail of the dragon. The trunk is of gigantic proportions being six feet between the shoulders. The ruins in white marble arround this spot cover a space of about five acres, and from the ship looks like a portion of snow on the ground. Looking towards the beach from the pedestal, on the right hand about four hundred yards is the remains of a dwelling house which has been discovered by the excavation of modern travellers—what renders this particularly curious is the colouring on the walls, in some places perfectly fresh. Further on in the same direction is the remains of a beautiful Amphitheatre in white marble, a great part of the flooring remains which is composed of the same material. For many years the Greeks of the adjacent islands have been in the habit of breaking up the marble in small portions and burning it in kilns as we do lime. Several of these kilns we saw prepared. But the Occupation of the Greek Revolution has so engaged the islanders in the wars with the Porte that this work as they call it has fallen into disuse. I saw an excavation which was made by some German travellers, where lay 5 fluted pillars of the portico to a small temple. Of the eight discovered, four had been removed by these gentlemen and put on board an Austrian frigate. In our research to day I saw several camelleons which were too quick in their motions to be captured. They seemed to live in sociability with vast quantities of Lizards. This island is seldom visited by the modern travellers. I am quite convinced that a great deal might be done here from excavation. A boy and girl whose occupation was to attend a few goats belonging to their master at Miceni were the only human beings on the island who made their appearance from their hiding place among the ruins. Having discovered some of the barge men put one of their goats into the boat, they came down to the beach followed by their favorite goat to claim his companion, which we restored and the two seamen on reaching the ship were reported for theft. However they disowned the charge by assuring the Commanding Officer that they supposed the animals were wild and belonged to the gentiles as much as the Turks.

This visit to Delos is typically recounted. One must remember that in Roehenstart's time archeology was in its infancy, and must not be surprised to find him, though using many of the standard books of his day on antiquities, falling into error. He erred along with most travelers in the pre-Schliemann period in thinking that the village of Bournabachi occupied the site of Homeric Troy. His confident belief in that location is stated firmly on his visit in 1819. Writing (in French) of the Scamander he says:

The plain that it waters is called "the flowery field of Scamander." It is described as having clear, pure water, whereas the Simois, coming down from the mountains, swollen by the accumulation of snows and the rains of autumn, rolls noisily its muddy waters and draws down in its rapid course rocks, trees, and dead bodies. Through lack of proper study several have been mistaken as to the site of Troy, but the precision of Homer is such that I do not believe he employed a single detail as to locality which even now is not perfectly applicable to the places he described. Some have pushed blindness so far as to say that the matter of the Iliad is pure fiction of the poet, and that the city of Troy in Asia Minor never existed except in the head of Homer! Mr. [Jacob] Bryant has published a work to support this hypothesis: the author is certainly a fool, or one of these beings who wish at all costs to build up a literary reputation no matter how and in maintaining the silliest notions. If it was possible to shake the truth of historical facts that have been transmitted to us by the ancients and that are contained in Homer; if it could ever be proved to me that we are all in the wrong as to this matter, I should for my part say, "Leave me my error: it makes me happy."

The plain of the Turkish village of Bournabachi coincides perfectly with that of Troy.

His interest in the Homeric scene lasted on, and in 1833 he spent days exploring the mounds and fields in the region of the Scamander and Simois. He seems from his notes to have done this exploring by himself alone, though at times he suddenly drops into a plural "we." The same peculiarity in psychological attitude is shown in his account of his journey on foot over the Alps to Geneva in 1815. He had then a companion but writes as if he were quite alone. Psychologically perhaps he was always alone, or at least aloof. He seldom speaks of his wife or of close companions. One can hardly believe that he went about the Troad without any guide, but his focus is always on himself, and he evidently reveled in being treated as a personage. The course of one day as reported by himself will show his ready adaptability to strange surroundings. He seldom complains of conditions unpleasant to travelers either in towns or in country regions. The space here given to Greek shepherds as compared with the temple of the Tymbrian Apollo reveals personal traits:

St. Vincent off the plain of Troy August 1833

Starting again yesterday, taking great care you may be sure to avoid the marsh, passing again through Kalefate and keeping more to the right than I did in my last visit, I soon reached the conical Tumulus and continuing my course along the mound mentioned by Dr. Clarke arrived at the temple in the grove of oak, where I found the Greek shepherds with their flocks had sought shelter from the mid-day sun and were just commencing their frugal meal, which consisted of brown bread and cucumber, a neighboring fountain supplying them as usual with a bountiful supply of cool spring water. They spread out their capote on which they invited me to be seated close to the fragment of a beautiful marble frieze, which served as a table on this occasion, on which was placed watermelon, cucumber, a few Colambydes, and the coarse brown barly bread of the mountains. While I was partaking of the welcome and hearty repast of these humble persons, I saw a stir that something was coming as a luxury. This was some curd cheese obtained from the Ewes, and which had been put in a bladder and cooled in the running stream. I never partook of any thing half so cooling and grateful. This was too great a luxury for themselves and was only for me. An old shepherd who presented it, eating a little himself as he placed it before me—pronouncing Callo-callo. I had the post of honor here assigned me. The capotes were rolled and some put under my head and arms, I was invited to be at my ease, when a cheboque was presented while I smoked the group seated in a circle around me, and the old patriarch looking father at my feet. I could not but admire the picture, the outer circle comprised the dogs each near his master lay enjoying the cool shade with a watchful eye towards the strangers, and around were the marble remains of the beautiful temple.

I had been that morning recommended to take a pocket pistol containing a little brandy. This I mixed in the calabash with a little water and handed it round, each applying his hand to his heart as he passed the cup exclaimed, Callo! Callo! Effendi, Callo! (Good my lord good).

The Greeks are very quick; pointing to the marble remains & giving them to understand that I was in search of ruins, they pointed to the north and constantly repeated Nero Nero Hali-El-Alli marmora marmora. I immediately knew that I was in the direction pointed out to cross a river, and that I should find marble at a village of Hali ali. In three hours I reached the river, and found myself near a Cellar in a grove of cypress trees, not far from which were the remains of the Temple dedicated to the Tymbrian Apollo. These villages are composed of wretched huts, built from the remains, and it is common to see the most beautiful fragments of white marble as a portion of the wall.

I returned by Kumquie: here the Turkish Agga invited me to his divan, and regaled me with coffee & a cheboque. I reached the ship at ten at night much fatigued and highly gratified.

Roehenstart's interest in antiquities, keen as it is, hardly exceeds his interest in men and women or in the manners of strange lands. His sociability and adaptability are important personal traits. Less indicative of his personality may seem to be the thumbnail sketches of famous persons whom he meets in his journeyings; but after all they illustrate his ability to find interesting events or interesting people. He happens to go ashore at Nauplia in August, 1832, on the day when grief at the funeral of the Greek patriot Ipsilanti engrosses the town. While at Egina he and his friends visited the heroic Canaris, and his story of the visit shows interest in the rites of hospitality and also in the person of Madame Canaris. He is very fond of describing the costumes of the Levantine ladies: one consequently wonders if perhaps some of these journals were letters to his wife.[1]

[1] At Smyrna Roehenstart expresses to Eki Effendi a wish that he might introduce the noble Turk to Mrs. Stuart: she "has left her country to follow the fortunes of her husband, that she was now at Malta, waiting my arrival."

While Roehenstart was absent from his lodging, Canaris had paid him a visit, and naturally the visit was returned:

The modern Themistocles was at home, seated with some masters of merchant-men who had been the companions of his youth. He was glad to see us, invited us to sit down—asked me very kindly after Sir Henry Hotham, and conversed on the subject of our journey. There was no introduction to his friends nor even to his lady, who entered followed by one of the young heros of Canaris's ship and who was a near kinsman to the Admiral. This young man bore a tray on which was a large glass of sweet jelly and spoons. Madam approaching us took the jelly in her hand and offering a spoon I helped myself, she then went round and returning to me took my spoon from me and presented me with a glass of water. This is the custom throughout the Levant, and is preparatory to coffee which she served herself. This is the greatest compliment that can be paid a stranger. Madam Canaris is about thirty—of a very fair complexion light hair and blue eyes. Her dress consisted on this occasion which I was given to understand was the usual dress of the morning of a green jacket lined with amber and ornamented with gold lace, a muslin handkerchief was thrown over the neck which was open and ornamented with a profusion of small gold beads. The tight sleeve of her jacket reached well below the elbow where it terminated in an open hanging slash fringed with a border of brochtra [trodtra?]. A pitticoat of amber silk trimmed with a pink boarder reached half way to the knee where a second of black fell trimmed with a great many rows of narrow yellow ribbon reach the calf, discovering the chemise trimmed with lace. This whole dress was bound together by a rich shawl round the waist, which answerd the purpose of stays, which the Greek women do not use. Her light hair of which she had a great profusion hang [*sic*] twisted below her shawl without ornament or curl. On the whole Madam Canaris is a fair beauty, like her husband simple and unaffected in her manners. Count Pecchio describes her grave and modest as Minerva. After we had smoked a cheboque, on our going away, she perfumed us with sweet water, followed us to the door where she stood till we were hid from her sight.

Canaris had asked us to dine, but we were anxious to visit the island and pleaded our excuse on this score.

Canaris, anxious to avenge some portion of the horrors committed at Scio, in an Ipsoanti [?] vessel charged with combustibles, disguised in such a manner as to resemble a merchantman bound for Smyrna, bore up for the Turkish fleet and passing the lookout vessels unmolested sailed boldly into the midst of the fleet at anchor in Scio roads; he succeeded in grappling his fire ship to a Turkish line of battle ship which bore the flag of the Caputan Pasha which he succeeded in destroying with the monster himself and the whole of his crew. Standing up in his boat, while the ship was in flames, he cryed out "Death to the moslimm, Tis I Canaris who did it."

From matters of costume to anecdotes of Byronic heroism the account is typical of Roehenstart's catholic tastes as a traveler. Wherever he is, he is always interested in persons of literary fame. Quarantined in 1832 at Egina he happens upon a lady made famous by Lord Byron:

> Mrs. Black also came to see her Husband She led a little boy of three years old—her only child. This lady was Miss Maeri, so celebrated as the Maid of Athens by Lord Byron. Poor Theresa, the death of her father and the long destructive war of her country has reduced her family to great poverty. The dark eyes and raven hair still show some remains of that beauty which captivated the youthful poet.

And again he writes:

> Went and spent the evening with Mrs. Black. Her husband Mr. Black is at present engaged on board the Russian squadron as a teacher of languages. He is a very handsome young man, a native of Colchester, much devoted to Greek literature and romantically devoted to the cause of Grecian independence.

Disillusioned ghosts of the past! The "Maid of Athens" married to a teacher of languages from Colchester!

In calling on the Maid of Athens he meets a famous French poet:

> In the house we also found Monsieur LaMartine the French poet, with his wife, who by the way, is our country woman no other than the daughter of Alderman Birch. They have one child—a girl of eleven years. I had been introduced to him by Sir Henry Hotham at Naplia where I had dined with him and met him afterwards. He has freighted at his own expense a vessel of 300 tons, and accompanied by Madam and daughter from this he intends first to visit Constantinople, then Jerusalem, Palmyra and Balbec if the Arabs will allow him—it being his object to pass into Egypt, ascend the Nile as far as Thebes. He is to winter at Smyrna, when he will visit the islands of the Archipelago and return home through Italy. Such he observes is the plan of his long and adventurous voyage. He does not calculate upon writing. "I go", he says, "to seek a purely personal inspiration on this great theatre of the religious and political events of the ancient world. I go to read before I die the finest pages of the material creation. If poetry should find them fertile in new inspirations and images I shall content myself in gathering them to colour a little the literary future which may remain for me." He is at present considered the first living poet. He has translated Child Harold and finished the remaining Canto. His poetry is much in the style of Byron—he is a remarkably genteel looking man, rather handsome, about thirty-six years of age. Altho he speaks English tolerably well, and understands it grammatically, yet he seems to prefer speaking French.

Scattered through his other travel journals also are similar accounts of writers, scholars, or statesmen, whom he met. He gives a long account of the Countess of Albany's friend, Alfieri; he discusses the merits of Rousseau's *Nouvelle Heloise* and other works as well. He even stoops to retail gossip about Mme de Staël:

Three leagues from Nyon is the chateau and village of Copette, the country of Mme de Staël. Since she had my promise to come to see her, I couldn't lose the opportunity of visiting this celebrated woman.—Nothing can convey the charm of her conversation: she has never been pretty, but her wit must have won her many conquests: her eyes and arms are very beautiful, and I readily imagine that she could still be preferred to many young and pretty women.—She is criticized for having lovers, but she is free and can follow her liking without wronging anyone. She lost her husband long since, and after all is it just to regard as criminal in a woman what is, so to speak, applauded in a man? One must only keep within measure and avoid scandal.—I have heard that her lover at the moment, successor to Benj. Constant, Labédoyère, Schleugel, and Conye[se] is a young man of Geneva, a M. de Rocca, who fought in Spain, where he was wounded and concerning which he has just published memoirs, which his mistress has *blanchi* before allowing them to be seen. She has, so they say, brought this handsome chevalier into a consumption, *bien en forme*. People are unjust and malicious: they like especially to tear down those who are out of the ordinary: it is thus that they give her for *bonne amie* an English demoiselle who lives with her; but this monstrous taste does not accord with a passion for men. One has to be careful not to accept the silly gossip of the public.

The chief members of her coterie were Lady Charlotte Campbell & her daughter, who is on the point of marrying Sir W[m]. Cumming Gordon, Sir G. Webb, of whom I heard a rather pleasant account as also of Lady Webb when I passed through Lyon, where he was held prisoner for 10 years, the pretty Barone de Menou.

Mme de Staël seems to have changed with regard to Buonaparte and is very critical of the politics of England, which she regards as *egoiste*. She was not happy about her journey to London &c.—She talks of going to visit Greece. Her father, M. de Necker, lives at Beaulieu.

This was set down in 1815—at least the marriage mentioned took place in September, 1815. His later travels frequently contain day-by-day accounts of pleasant small adventures, such as we have already seen with the Greek shepherds. To return to the Near East we may again see his ready delight in a somewhat longer narrative of a day passed near Constantinople. The time was July, 1833:

Having learnt through the kindness of our little neighbour that the Grand Segnor was to inspect the Russian encampment in the afternoon, we determined to occupy the early part of the day in visiting the environs of the forest of Belgrade, opposite to which on the asiatic shore stands a sort of park called the Sultan's vally, the spot where the review was to take place, a distance of twelve miles from the city. The cracking of whips [by] our Tartar guides announced the arrival of our horses, and shortly after daylight our party were seated in the saddle, mounting the hill outside of the town. It is on the acclivity of this hill where stands the famous fountain which receives the waters in pipes from the aqueduct, and from hence branches of the pipes to supply the four quarters of the city.

From this our road conducted us four miles over an uncultivated rocky hill where scarcely a blade of grass is to be seen. This dreary sight was amply repaid as our horses winded slowly down the abrupt declivity which terminated this rugged hill. A valley of considerable extent lay at our feet ornamented with some farms enclosed by hedges, a thing which I have no where found before in the Levant. These farms guard the browsing of a thousand flocks. The sheep are the african breed; the coats weigh from 30 to 40 lbs. The plough was also in action by four oxen, and made a tollerable deep furrow (ploughing in manure) a circumstance also but rarely to be seen on the shores of the Mediterranean. The usual custom being to leave the land fallow for a season and then sow it, either with wheat or barley, or indean corn. There was also a small shew of the cotton plant on each of the farms, with the usual portion of watermelons and cucumbers and cabbages, which comprises the chief food of the peasantry. Rich meadows carpeted the centre of this beautiful vally wattered by the windings of a considerable stream, and afforded pasture to many herds of oxen of a grey colour, not large but very fat.

No hour at this season in these climates is so soft and so cheering to the spirits than sunrise. The picture was beautiful, and our admiration was considerably heightened in viewing the great Forest of Belgrade, the object of our visit, spreading its dark thick foliage for miles over the hills and dells which terminated the distance. Another hour along the valley brought us to the skirts of the forest which we penetrated by a bridle road truly romantic, ascending and descending alternately over precipices and rocks covered and surrounded with valonnia oaks and immense groves of chesnut trees. All at once we came on the village of Belgrade, which stands on a spacious opening in the forest. Here our Tartar guide and the french servant prepared a breakfast, consisting of coffee, eggs and cream, not unlike that which is potted in Devonshire. This repast while we were walking about was spread out on the grass under the large trees which overhang a small fountain. This is still pointed out as a favorite spot of our fair country woman Lady M. W. Montagu, as well as her residence, an old wooden house painted red, which with its garden is now fast going into decay. It was from this very house that she gave Europe these elegant epistles that in her day and still in our own are so much and so deservedly admired.[1]

[1] Roehenstart at this point inserts a marginal note saying: "Here ends Mrs. A. Brunurn's letter 20 Sept. 1833."

Mr. Black, one of our first Turky merchants has his country house in this village. . . . [They briefly visit Mr. Black.]

Taking leave of our countryman, we persued a new direction through the forest that still presented the same romantic undulating scenery—the lofty trees affording a refreshing shade from the powerful rays of the mid-day sun delighted the horses and sharpened the wit of our Tartar guide, whose mountebank tricks and jokes over the poor half witted greek lad, in charge of the horses, were truly ridiculous. We soon reached the grand Acqueduct whose arches still conduct the waters from the reservoirs to Constantinople, a distance of fourteen miles, one of the great works of the magnificent Sultan Solyman. A little farther on and we had a charming view. Close to our left run a deep cultivated valley from the forest to the shore of the Bosphorus, where stood the village of Buyukdéré, its houses and gardens skirting its deep bay, were ornamented by the streamers and masts of the Russian fleet. The Armenian village of Tarapia, the favorite country residence of the foreign ambassadors lay at our feet washed by the Bosphorus, whose width scarcely a mile, devides the two continents. The hills immediately in front on the opposite shore were speckled with the white and green tents of the Russian and Turkish encampments. On our left the towering hills and opening of the Black Sea, to the right the sea of Marmora and the distant view of the Olympian range.

Scarcely had we seated ourselves in the boats which were to conduct us over to the Sultans vally, than the sound of artillery anounced the appearance of the imperial yaucht, a beautiful and highly ornamented steam vessel built in Scotland. In a few minutes we reached the asiatic shore and got well placed on the small pier where his highness was to land. As he descended from the steamer into the barge the three frigates of the Allied powers, moored midway in the stream, manned yards and fired a royal salute of twenty-one guns each. I assure you that no words of mine can adequately express the splendour, the elegant light taste of the imperial barge. Her ornaments are costly, yet far from being overloaded, and entirely of a different dunn from the boats of the Lord Mayor. This boat is ninety feet long, pulls double banked by a crew of twenty powerful men, dressed in red caps, wide sleeved shirts of white silk with loose Turkish blouses of white cotton and yellow slippers. The floor of the stern sheets is covered with a red English carpetry made I understand expressly for the purpose. The Sultan was seated on a crimson sofa close to the stern, elevated a little above those at the sides which were occupied by the Sereinker [?] Pasha, Caputan Pashaw and several members of the Divan, all clad in the new military dress after the fashion of the continental armies, and wearing the Star and cressent composed of the most beautiful and brilliant diamonds.

In stepping from his barge, finding himself surrounded by the vast staff and officers of the Russian fleet, Mahmoud hesitated for a few seconds, looked around, like one doubtful whether to approach or not. It struck me that this embarrassment might have arisen from the cold and uncourtous manners of the Muscovites, who never left [lift?] the hat but to their Emperor, a stupid silence was observed, nor bow or obesence made. The approach of Count Orloff with his Dragoman recalled his Highness to himself and placing his hand upon his breast, assured His Excellency that he had great pleasure in visiting the camp of his good friends. The count conducted his Highness to the head of the pier, where the Pashas and Ottoman Staff were in waiting. Here the Sultan mounted a beautiful little Arab from a stone horse-block, the usual mode observed on state occasions. To an English equestrian nothing can appear more awkward than this ceremony. Drawing up the shoulders and cloak, pointing the elbows at right angles with the body, two of the Pashas lay hold of his highness with both hands under the arm and actually push him up the steps, a page on each side hold the stirrup and continued to walk one at the horses head, which from time to time they continued to pat and stroke: the effect of this imperial mounting was altogether the most unbecoming ceremony you can fancy. The Pageant proceeded up the valley followed by a splendid retinue mounted on beautiful Arabs.

His Highness was received by the Russian army with presented arms, a salute of cannon, music and drums. He then proceeded to a tent on the acclivity of the hill in front, from whence he viewed the movements of the Russian line. The Russians move with continuous and great precision and seem to confine their movements to an exact well ordered and compact march in line. The Review this day consisted of four thousand infantry two hundred horse, and two brigades of Artillery. As soon as the Sultan had taken his place, the troops changed position to the left—by echellon forming two lines. Skirmishers out in front were drove back when the first line advanced and opened a fire. The second line advanced in double column and relieved the first, passing the centre in Column of companies & deploying on a centre through the centre. This movement was done in great precision, under the cover of salvoes from the whole Artillery. The second line resting in line, ordered arms and stood easy. The two lines threw themselves into two squares the Guns occupying the left face of the first, and the right of the second. The line was formd to their former [state] to the left of the valley. The Sultan was again received with a general salute. The line advanced, and broke into Col quarter distance right in front, and defiled before his Highness to their various stations on the heights. This terminated the review. The Cavalcade again returned to the Blocking Stone, dismounted, embarked and descended the Bosphorus under a 2d salute from the allied frigates.

At the presentation of the officers Mahmoud observed a very young man commanding one of the regiments and who carried two decorations—said You are very young for your rank? where did you gain these decorations—From my sovereign your Highness.—In what battle? In a battle fought with one of our most valliant enemies, who happily has become now our dearest friend, Your Highness. Mahmoud was much pleased and beg the young soldier would permit him to have the honorable decorations set in diamonds.

Still another aspect of Roehenstart's almost juvenile readiness to enjoy life is seen when on board the "St. Vincent" at Smyrna in 1833 he received visitors or paid visits ashore:

The Ship having anchored so near the town has occasioned much interest to the whole of the inhabitation whose curiosity has been considerably excited by the reports made and magnified by those who paid us a visit the first day. So large a ship has never before been seen at Smyrna. The variety of dress to be seen on our quarter deck from six in the morning till ten o'clock was highly gratifying, for at Constantinople, where the new system works well, the Nobles and frequenters of the Court had thrown aside the Turban & ample Eastern Robes. But here where they are so far removed from the Court, it is only a few of the Government Officers and those in public employments who have been compelled to submit to the national degradation of assuming the dress of infidels. The Greeks are fond of visiting the ship, and come off in great numbers, the father, mother, and the whole families. The girls are fond of our military band and with the greatest simplicity stand up to dance; so that our young midshipmen have as much practice at this salutary and accomplished exercise as they had last year with the Spanish maidens. That part of the female dress, which formerly attracted so much the admiration of travellers and which was constituted the habilment of the Smyrneotes has now given way to the European costume. Still we frequently saw the Oriental dress which certainly is interesting: it consists of loose trousers which reach to the ancle and shows off the little foot to great advantage, the little jacket of silk and velvet which left the lower part of the arm bare, and which is encircled by clasps of gold and numerous ornaments, these were principally worn by the families who came from the country to visit the great ship. These ladies are in general ornamented with a beautiful head of black hair tied up in tresses, which fall over the shoulders accorded with pink and blue ribbon, a portion is encircled round the top of the head, with flowers feathers and jewels, the neck and the bosom is always open....

The Turks are an odd sedate people. After walking round the ship with Eki Effendi, one of the first gentlemen of the place, we reached the quarter deck just at the moment that a group of our midshipmen were figuring away in the dance under the awning. The curiosity and pleasure he experienced, at seeing the ship and squatting himself down cross-legged on the deck fixed his eyes with the greatest astonishment, and directing his pipe-bearer to seek for his friends who had loitered behind on the deck to come, instantly, or they might lose the sight of the dancers. They soon arrived and squatting down were equally delighted and pleased with the novelty of the scene. Eki Effendi then told me that they hired the greeks from the Islands to dance before them at their weddings and festivities. Having witnessed the first quadril [he] added that the young gentlemen had danced long enough, that he was much pleased and begged they would take care of themselves after so violent an exertion.

A Turkish gentleman approaching me on deck addressing me in french in the best parisian style acquainted me that he had been directed to introduce himself to Captain Ballingall, that he had taken the liberty in common with his countrymen to intrude with a party of friends to visit the ship. This person was the only one of the party dressed after the *new system*, and it immediately struck me from the fluency of his language that he was a renegade frenchman. I found him very polite. I conducted the whole party round the ship. I showed him my little cabin and my books, offered him some refreshment &c. with which he and the whole party was much pleased. On his taking leave he assured me how much he and the whole party were pleased with the attentions I had been pleased to shew them. He then acquainted me that he was the son of the Molloch of Smyrna, and that the gentleman in the Turkish costume was his senior brother, the chief judge of the city who had requested him to say that he would consider it a compliment if I would honor him with a visit and added that he would request Dr. Clarke to accompany me to his house, where he would have much pleasure to introduce me to his father. I assured him that I should do myself the honor, and most certainly avail myself of his polite invitation.

Yesterday I started to pay my visit. Dr. Clarke unfortunately had gone into the country, but Mrs. Clarke said I should not be disappointed in my intended visit. For I was to consider it a great honor to receive an invitation to the house of the Molla. She requested Mr. and Mrs. Purdy, an American merchant and his wife, with Mr. Wooly, an English merchant of eminence to join the party, Dr. Sinclair, herself and her two interesting pretty daughters, girls of 12 to accompany us. On our way Mrs. Clark said she would pass through the garden of Eki Effendi, the little Turk, who was so delighted at the dancing the day before. It would save a considerable walk, and that she could take that liberty, for we might have a peep of the ladies if they happened to be in the garden. We entered the garden which we traversed without seeing other than the gardeners and servants loitering about the Courtyard of a great staircase. We had scarcely left the gate on the other side when a black eunuch came running after us to say that the ladies were sorry we should pass without taking some refreshment, and begged we would return. This was just what Mrs. Clarke wished, and was at that moment regretting that the ladies had not seen our party. On entering the great gate which on this occasion was opened for our convenience, Eki Effendi himself received us, and conducted the party to his Kioski in the garden near the foot of the great stairs. This is what our good people in England would call a temple to be seen sometimes in the gardens of our Noblemen. An open apartment in the stile of the pictures which we frequently see in the Ladies pocket Book, representing the Brighton Palace. An ornamental roof supported with columns of light filagreed work. You enter this elegant apartment by a flight of a few steps in imitation of an ancient temple. The floor is of marble; in the centre is a fountain and jet d'eau surrounded with beautiful flowers, watered and cherished by a stout beardless etheopean, whose sole pleasure in this life is to arrange this apartment, to cherish his flowers, and to receive the thanks of the beauties of the harem. We had scarcely taken our places in the divan when a second beardless black announced in a squeaky voice that it was the pleasure of the harem to see the ladies. As our fair country women rose to go, we involuntarily rose to bow to the ladies. Poor Eki Effendi, unaccustomed to this part of European manners, was evidently embarrassed and requested our interpreter, who on this occasion was Mr. Purdy, to explain to us that he was extremely sorry, the custom of his country prohibited gentlemen going up stairs, that it was the ladies alone who were requested to do the harem that honor . . . he conducted the ladies of our party towards the door of the Harem. Two black servants brought us sherbet from the harem with the compliments that the ladies had prepared our sherbet with their own hands. . . .

There was a party of us 6 gentlemen, and 6 attendants appeared bringing each a pipe which they presented after the ladies sent us sweet jelly and water. As I reclined smoking my cheboque, a gentleman was announced who had arrived from the interior, a merchant of some repute in the interior of Asia Minor. He was quite astonished to find his old friend's divan filled with so many franks [Europeans]. He was an excessively handsome man, with an extraordinary full bushy black beard about thirty six years of age. As he ascended the few steps he slipped off his shoes, and saluting the whole company sat down on the divan and before saying a word smoked a pipe.

Coffee was served in little china cups which rested in one of filagree of silver somewhat in the shape of an egg cup. The ladies returned in half an hour and said that they had been highly gratified with their visit. . . . After the ladies returned, the blacks again appeared with a second beverage of red sherbet. On taking our leave the stranger who sat at his pipe unmoved desired the interruption to say that he knew I was a gentleman of consequence from my manner. This brought out one of my best bows you be may sure as we took our leave.

Our next visit was to the Mollah. Here we were received by my french friend who had been looking out for us. We passed into the garden, or rather into a grove of pomgranate, orange, and lemon trees, the walks being laid out at right angles. In the centre a little elevated stood a magnificent Kioski of lofty dimentions having a stream of water beneath filled with gold and silver fish, with a rocky island in the centre clothed with some pretty plants. In the Kioski sat the old Molah, a fine old man whose gray beard reached below his chest. He made me sit by him, and I received his pipe. He seemed highly amused to hear his son conversing with me in a foreign language. At one end of this apartment was a jet d'eau ellegantly cut in white marble. Iced water, sweetmeats, coffee & pipes constituted our entertainment, washing hands with rose water before we left to walk in the garden. During this time our amiable companions were invited into the harem. While walking in the garden I was diverted with several storks, whose sagaceous look and awkward gait attracted my notice. Every now and then a turtle flew across the path. The old gentleman seeing that this pleased me clapped his hands, which caused flocks of these doves to leave the thick foliage. Under the trees was some gazelles perfectly tame following us for the sweet meats. This was the garden belonging to the harem; that for the gentlemen was plain and divided by a wall. Here eight beautiful little arab horses were racked up under some trees: each had a short line attached to his hind feet; their beds were made of chopped hay in the shape and manner in which our gardeners form the beds for radishes. One of these little horses was the greatest beauty I ever saw—brown with dark main and tail. I played with him for sometime, and on coming away I was told as I admired the little arab that he was mine and that I might have him to take to England. As it is usual in the East if you accept a present to give one in return, I had nothing with me that was at all equivalent. So I thanked His Grace, assuring him how sensible I was of his kindness, but situated as I was, not knowing how political affairs would lead us, I was afraid that some accident might occur to him. However, they were determined that I should take something, so they presented me one of the little gazelles. The harem at this house consisted of the wife and daughter in law of the old judge—with some few young women and a child or two. They were very polite, but not so gay as the ladies at Eki Effendi's.

I was quite astonished to see the number of pets the ladies had—goats, antelopes, and numerous flocks of Durtle Doves who were at liberty to fly and build their nests in every tree. But I was astonished to learn that the whole establishment had only arrived that morning from their estate in the country.

Such accounts have a charm in their revelation of a fundamentally enjoying personality. His sympathies go even further than those exhibited in his accounts of men and women. He gets sentimental and affectionate repeatedly with regard to animals. Those mentioned in the Mollah's gardens illustrate the fact, but Roehenstart speaks kindly even of normally less attractive animals. He is not distressed by the dogs that infest the streets of Constantinople; he waxes eloquent on Paros concerning the utility of the "noble" ass, and he is delighted by the affection and obedience that camels show to their masters. Greatly impressed with these last animals at Smyrna, he gives the following account of them:

It is here that the European traveller is struck with the wonderful number of camels that are continually to be seen in ranks one after the other entering the town with loads of merchandise from and to the interior. The sight is beyond anything extraordinary to a person from England who has been accustomed to see the articles of merchandise conveyed by canal or in our ponderous broad wheeled wagons on roads constructed at great expense. The whole commerce of Asia Minor is carried by means of these animals under a burning sun and upon an arid soil, enduring great fatigue, sometimes without food for days, and seldom completely slaking his thirst more than once or twice during a progress of several hundred miles. Yet this noble creature under such privations is patient, apparently happy, and charmed with the kind expressions of his dervidge, or owner, at whose command he [or] they kneel down to receive their burden, in general a weight of six or seven hundred weight.

When the load is properly adjusted the animal rises and at command falls into his rank; for they always march in single file. Unlike the lean and feeble animals that we now and then see led about our streets, we here behold a noble huge creature with his head erect, stepping gracefully and without the least noise or fear through a crowded city. I always stop with pleasure to behold these patient sensible creatures pass along.

It is really truly curious to see them arrive at the spot where they are to deposit their burden. They halt and front at the command of their master with the greatest exactness. The camel on the left is then commanded to lay down, and when eased of his load rises and cheerfully takes his place on the right while the next performs his duty equally exact, and so on till the whole are released. Each dervidge has generally twelve of them in charge. They walk in file preceeded by an ass saddled for the convenience of the dervidge. It is really delightful to observe the groups when all released from their duties the dervidge sets down and shares his brown loaf with his companions of the desert, giving his favorite who is by his side a little more than the rest, who seems proud of the superior attention of his master. I am not ashamed to tell you that at the close of this picture, I was really moved to see this sensible, this patient, this noble creature come, kneel before his master, inviting him by the most affectionate regards to mount. The poor and hardy dervidge patted the noble creature, and told him in a language that they both understood that he would ride the ass. No sooner had he mounted than the noble creature again invited him to dismount. The dervidge seeing that I was pleased, desired the creature to come to him, and holding up his chin the animal actually rubbed his face over his head and shoulders, and seemed delighted with the caress of his master. Down he went soliciting a third time for his master to mount. All three had been equally delighted, the Turk, the camel, and myself. . . .

The silence of their step is one of the most curious features in the history of the camel. Not the least clank or noise is heard. You see whole rows of them coming down the streets of Smyrna heavily laden with immense bags of wool, which adds to their immense size, with as little noise as that made by a dog.

There is a charm in Roehenstart's perceptions and sympathies, even when at times his prose becomes wavering and chaotic. One should always remember that these excerpts come from drafts of letters, much and yet incompletely revised. The spelling (here for the most part silently corrected) is more defective than in his more careful writing. At times he violates English idiom noticeably: he wrote as well as spoke English "with an accent." But in travel he seems to forget the wrongs under which he suffers, and becomes a cheerful, likable person —a man of intelligence and of quick sympathy.

CHAPTER TEN

Last Journeyings

After the mid-thirties we have few papers and little information about Roehenstart. Naturally he was exasperated by the increasingly frequent mentions in the public press of the romantic "Sobieski Stuarts." In the summer of 1836 a paragraph about them that he saw in *Galignani's Messenger* spurred him to adverse comment on these rival pretenders to Stuart blood. He sent his observations to the *Glasgow Chronicle*, which naturally refused to publish the communication because of its anonymity. After the intervention of a friendly agent, a nephew of Mrs. Harriet Hamilton, it was printed. In August, 1836, he had sent the piece to his wife in a very friendly letter addressed to "Madame Stuart, rue du Harley No. 4 au Marais, Paris." Since this is the last mention of Mrs. Stuart in the papers preserved to us, the letter may be given in full. The lady must have predeceased her husband: there is no evidence in the matter except silence. The letter reads as follows:

Here I send you, my dearest Constance, a copy of the Article I alluded to in my last, premising that I was almost compelled to write it. As I had no one who could act for me, I was obliged to address the Editor myself: this accounts for the little praise I threw in to disguise the writer. I saw in Galignani's a paragraph, copied from a Scotch paper, giving an account of a visit paid to Scotland by two young men, brothers, one Chs Edward, the other John Sobieski, represented in glowing colours &c &c. I felt certainly ruffled, and having made up my mind not to stir any more in this melancholy business, I would not have taken any further notice of the paragraph if I had not been teazed into compliance. There must be an answer to my letter, and you shall know it, when I get it, which I think will be before we go from hence.

To the Editor of the Glasgow Chronicle

SIR:—Feeling deeply interested in every circumstance relating to the unfortunate House of the Stuarts, my attention has been attracted from time to

time by various articles, which have appeared in different papers, all calculated to mislead public opinion. One of these paragraphs, to which I allude, was transcribed from the Glasgow Chronicle into Galignani's Messenger of the 14th of may last. I should feel much obliged if you could inform me, thro' the medium of your paper who are those "Two young men dressed in the Highland Costume, accompanied by a Piper" who have lately been paying a visit to Scotland. I perceive that their claim does not rise above illegitimacy, and even to such a pretension I must object, knowing as I do the private history of that illustrious Family. The only person who claimed this spurious descent was Mr Stuart Hall who, after having made his fortune in India, returned to Scotland, and this Gentleman designated himself as the son of Cardinal York. It is a fact well known that Prince Charles Edward had by his first marriage, only one child, a Daughter, the Duchess of Albany,—he had no issue by his second marriage with the late Countess of Albany, well known as the mistress of Alfieri:—the Prince had no natural child. This Daughter, the Duchess of Albany, married a Nobleman descended in a direct line from the Earl of Darnley, husband to Mary, Queen of Scots. This union was kept secret on account of his being a Protestant, but on the birth of a son, the marriage was disclosed to Prince Chas Edward, who not only pardoned his daughter, but gave his own name to the boy. This grandson, the only remaining scion of the Stuarts, whom I have known almost from his birth, unites both branches of the Stuarts, and is living in comparative poverty and complete retirement. He has been the sport of that cruel destiny which has so relentlessly weighed upon his family with an iron hand, but he soars above life's frowns with a dignity becoming his Royal race, and a fortitude worthy of a better fate. Sir, your inserting this letter in your Chronicle will oblige,—A Scotsman.
Naples June 18 1836.

Many thanks for your kind letter, my dear Friend [Constance]; it arrived on the 27th July, and I have lost one courier, that I might inform you of R's answer. All's right; the money has been paid this morning. My letters ought to reach you much sooner than yours arrive to me, since they are intrusted to the master of a Barge, who is an honest man, and put into the post office at Naples, as this shall be to morrow morning, being the post day; I cannot account for the great delay you complain of. The postage of yr letters is more than double that which you pay for mine, and English letters do not pay half as much. I knew all about the King, and the news you communicate, even to Mdlle Garnerin, also the great heat you suffer at Paris, since I continue to read G's paper, twenty days old.

I am sorry to hear the Cholera is raging at Vienna, and nearer us, in the north of Italy, at Venice &c. They have already reestablished the Quarantine here, no, they would not let escape such a good opportunity of plaguing and plundering Travellers. The Italians are persuaded that it is contagious: I have not found it so last year at Genoa; but when I reflect that they are great cowards, the experience I have of this strange and as yet little understood malady induces me to believe that with them it may be in many instances contagious, for I am convinced that wherever it rages, those who tremble, are most liable to fall victims to the Cholera.

Should you wish to write, contrive it so that your letter may reach me in the early part of September, for our time is out on the 15th, and I hope we shall not prolong our stay here. The only inducement for coming to Sorrento during the hot weather is that the place is free from moschettos: true we have none, but we have plenty of little black flies, called sunflies, or I believe modges [*sic*] in England, and another specie of gnat, much smaller than the usual, and fully as troublesome. I am all covered with their sting, and they annoy me beyond expression: hardly any night passes away without my having the fever, so very maddening they are: partial as I am to Italy, I trust this will be the last summer I ever pass in it. You may rely on my writing you before we leave Sorrento, and when I know our further proceedings. The green tea, I find, is a most excellent remedy, and it is owing to bad management if it did not answer with y.r friend—nonsense about the bad smell! There is no such thing. Let me end my letter by bringing back to your mind a very good resolution I heard you take *several times*, but which I have not had the pleasure yet of seeing you adopt: I had quite forgotten to mention it before:—it is to take lessons of French, not to speak it, because you do it indeed very well, and y.r pronunciation is good, but to enable you to write the language correctly: for you must have found most distressing not to be able to do it when required. I shall expect in your letter half a sheet of French as a specimen of y.r progress.

Ever truly and sincerely yours

STUART.

1st Aug.st 1836.

Ultimately (June 7, 1838) the *Glasgow Chronicle* printed the communication copied into this letter, with two or three modifications seemingly due to Roehenstart himself. To his request for the identification of the "Two young men . . . who have been paying a visit to Scotland" he added the caustic phrase, "and made themselves so conspicuous." He thought better of becoming a descendant of Darnley and inserted the preferable "descended in a direct line from James Moray Stuart, uncle of Darnley." He also improved the status of his fictitious father by adding after the story that "Prince Charles Edward . . . gave his name to the boy" the fantastic statement that the father "had fully satisfied the Prince that he possessed strong claims to consider himself as belonging to, if not the elder branch of the Royal Stuarts, and amongst old documents religiously preserved in his family, one of them bearing date of January, 927, proves that his ancestors were then, at that early period, Lords of Sutherland and the Orkney

Isles." Though grammatically incoherent this addendum was doubtless designed to put mere "Sobieski Stuarts" in their proper place. In the text sent to Mrs. Stuart one word appears coyly—perhaps humorously inserted—when Roehenstart, writing anonymously about himself asserts that he has known the grandson *almost* from his birth. The printed text lacks *almost*.

Notably in this major outburst against the Sobieski Stuarts, Roehenstart devotes more space to his own claims than to theirs. Consequently it may be interesting to see what they said about him. Nowhere in his papers does Roehenstart indicate that he ever saw the Ossianic brothers, but the aged surviving brother, then styling himself "Charles Edward Stolberg Sobieski Stuart, Comte d'Albanie" (his real name was Charles Manning Allen), in 1877 sent an anonymous communication to *Notes & Queries* which was there published in the issue for November 3, 1877. In part it reads:

> With regard to descendants of Clementina Walkinshaw, I may mention one (the last) with whom I was personally acquainted for some years before his death, and that was a Baron Rohenstart, a Swedish nobleman, who was said to be a grandson of Clementina Walkinshaw, and I have no reason to believe that he was not, whose father Baron Rohenstart, it was stated, was married to the daughter of Clementina Walkinshaw, which also I have no reason to doubt. Their son bore the names (as Christian names) of Charles Edward Stuart prefixed to his own family name of Rohenstart, which also I see no reason to dispute. He was first introduced to me as Baron Rohenstart in Prague, in the Casino, the club of the nobles of Bohemia, of which he was also a member. But he never assumed the title of Count of Albany. Had he assumed any title from his mother, it must have been Duke of Albany . . . but . . . Baron Rohenstart . . . was contented with the title which he inherited from his father. . . .
>
> Baron Rohenstart, who died from injuries caused by the upsetting of a stagecoach in which he was travelling from Edinburgh to Inverness . . . was the same as stated above. . . . How in the inscription on his tomb he came to be called Count Rohenstart I cannot understand. . . . During my acquaintance with him we often conversed about Scotland; and as he had been accustomed to visit that country from time to time, we talked frequently about its history (which was generally brought about by me, as I had heard, many years before I became acquainted with him, that he was the grandson of Clementina Walkinshaw, though delicacy prevented me from touching on that subject, as he did not; neither did he ever allude to his relationship with the Stuart family or to the fact that he bore as Christian names Charles Edward Stuart).

There is nothing clearly impossible in this account, though one feels the extent of the acquaintance is much exaggerated. It seems improbable that these two pretenders could converse often and long without touching on the one subject that really interested them: Scotland was all very well as a topic, but from Scotland one would naturally go on to the real matter. After all the aged Allen was seventy-eight years old when he wrote this communication, and Roehenstart had been dead over twenty years.

But in 1838 he was not dead, and since in his letter to his wife he remarks, that he had made up his mind "not to stir any more in this melancholy business," he may in later years have made it less a subject of conversation. It must have been in later years and in England or Scotland that he knew the surviving (second) grandson of Admiral Allen: he may of course have met him in Prague, but Prague is nowhere mentioned in Roehenstart's papers.

In these later years his closest friend was perhaps Charles Harrison of 9 Berkeley Street, Berkeley Square, whose house became (briefly?) Roehenstart's address in April, 1838. After about this time he preserved practically no personal papers except paragraphs sent to periodicals about Stuarts, actual or imaginary—a fact that suggests no decrease of interest in his ancestry. At the end of his life he was still traveling. He had studied a bit of Spanish and went off to Spain to see the country and collect pictures. His last letter, preserved in a draft, is to Charles Harrison, and it was written after Harrison's daughter. Frances Maria, had on July 27, 1853, become the wife of Lord Amelius Beauclerk, a younger son of the eighth Duke of St. Albans. The handwriting is more tremulous than usual, but the letter shows the eager, active, and forward-looking attitude of the writer:

FONDA DEL ORIENTE BARCELONA 13th May [1854]

MY DEAR CHARLES:—I must trouble you again with another of my epistles before I shall have the pleasure of meeting you. I duly received your kind letter directed to Valencia, and both yours & that of my dear cousin Lord Amelius, afforded me great satisfaction, although I must observe that you make too much of a thing which came of course & naturally, and did hardly deserve being mentioned. I had requested L. A. to tell me the state the oranges arrived in; and his silence on the subject proves that this was a failure: I am very sorry for it: but there is no mending the thing this year; I only trust that the same disappointment did not happen with the wine and that you did receive the quality I had selected.—I forgot to mention that they do not allow any letter to be paid in Spain for England, & therefore your last letter was paid twice.—

Pray write me a short note, and if you are too much engaged, I request L. A. to do it for you, acquainting me with your plan that I may act accordingly, and direct it to Hotel Beauvau, Marseille. 'Tis very strange, but we were all three engaged in the same pursuit at the same time. I mean the search after pictures. I have seen many surpassingly fine, splendid beyond all descriptions, and you will no doubt be surprised to hear me give the decided preference to the Madrid Museum over that of Paris! The Spanish School is extremely rich and hardly known either in France or England.—I have been very lucky in my ferretings, and I have actually laid my hand upon a Murillo which I paid extremely cheap, not one tenth of its value.—Two days after my purchase, I was offered $2500 piastres fortes which I did not accept; perhaps I was wrong! we shall see later.—What do you think of all my expenses being largely repaid, and having besides above £500 clear profit,—I have a pretty addition to make to both of your collections: however you must not expect anything in the style of Murillo:—they are modern but excellent cabinet pictures of the costumes & manners of Andalusia.

I have been unwell for above one week; but I am now quite recovered: 4 days & as many nights on the road (and what roads) had done for me, and my old bones could not bear it any longer. This is about the time I had fixed for leaving Spain, and I intend taking my passage by the next steamer to Marseille in about 4 or 5 days. I must go instantly to Nice to pay a last visit to a dying friend, and as I fancy that the German waters may do me some good, I think of proceeding straight on from Nice to Baden Baden, where I may remain a fortnight nursing myself a little, and then I shall move on to give you the meeting wherever you choose to fix it for that relaxation from business which you must want sadly. Recollect, I beg, that should you find necessary to give up for this year your excursion on the continent, this will equally please me, and I shall cross the sea from Ostend to join you in England, where they [*sic*] are many attractive spots to spend 6 weeks or 2 months in a charming way, besides auld Scotland all over which I should feel happy to chaperon you.—The little alteration I am obliged to make cannot in the least interfere with you, since your time is not yet up, and I am afraid there is no chance of your stirring before July, even perhaps as late as the end of August. Then dear Lady A's interesting situation may detain you in town longer than you thought. I merely mention all these casualties to prove that my going so early in the season to a watering place cannot in any manner interfere with your project, and should it jar with anything you have resolved, I am sure I would give up with pleasure everything of mine in order to meet you on your own ground.—I had so many things to communicate, and I do not recollect now any more, besides 'tis time I should bid you adieu. With my best regards to all your circle, I remain most sincerely yours

Stu

When this letter was written Roehenstart, though naturally unaware of the fact, had slightly less than six months to live. Evidently the meeting with Harrison did not take place on the Continent, for late in October Roehenstart with friends was riding on the top of a coach near the town of Dunkeld. A wheel came off, the coach overturned, and the fall was fatal to Roehenstart. He survived for a few days apparently, and seemed to improve, but collapsed and died on October 28. His friends had him buried in the tranquil grassy nave of the ruined cathedral of Dunkeld, and placed on his stone the following inscription:

SACRED
TO THE MEMORY OF
GENERAL
CHARLES EDWARD STUART
COUNT ROEHENSTART
WHO DIED AT DUNKELD
ON THE 28TH OCTOBER 1854
AGED 73 YEARS
SIC TRANSIT GLORIA MUNDI

Roehenstart was a colonel, but not a general, and one may doubt if he was more than seventy years old. One must assume that the friend who designed the stone (Charles Harrison?) was not perfectly informed as to many details of Roehenstart's life.

Before going to Spain Roehenstart had sketched out a last will for himself, and a copy of it, preserved among his papers, reads as follows:

This is the last Will and Testament of Charles Edward Stuart, Count of Roehenstart, now residing at No. 7 Cambridge Square, Hyde Park, London.

I give and bequeath to my friend Charles Harrison, Esquire, all my fortune and effects whatsoever in England & France, and I make him Executor of this my will, subject to the following bequests:

I give to the first born child of Lady Amelius Wentworth Beauclerk One Thousand Pounds Sterling, and should the said child die before he or she becomes of age, then the said sum of One Thousand Pounds, is to go to the next child and so on.

I give to Mrs. Margaret Hughes Five Hundred Pounds Sterling.

I give to Elizabeth Constance White Two Hundred Pounds Sterling.

I request Mr. Harrison to pay to Colonel Julien and his wife of No. 9 Rue Ne De de Lorette, Paris, Twenty Pounds Sterling, free from duty, to buy a little remembrance of me. They have taken charge of Two large Trunks & two small boxes belonging to me, containing Books, some plate, old rings & other valuable things, which they will deliver to Mr. Harrison.

I also wish him to pay for the same purpose and free from duty Twenty Pounds to Madame Dafour [Dufour?], wife of Dr. Dafour, rue Lamartine No. 46 Paris.

My papers are to be burnt, but particularly two sealed Parcels marked "*to be burnt at my death*."

This is my will, to which (written with my own hand) I have subscribed my name this Twenty ninth day of December one Thousand Eight Hundred and fifty-three. C. E. S.

Count of Roeh——

The papers were perhaps not all preserved, but they were not all burned. They evidently descended to Harrison's only daughter, who after the death of her first husband, Lord Amelius Beauclerk, later married General John Walpole D'Oyley. She died in 1910, and the papers were sold at Sotheby's in 1935.

The death of Roehenstart was briefly noticed in various newspapers. Practically no information concerning him was included except some mention of military rank and of his claim to be descended from Prince Charles Edward. The lack of information led to the following comment printed in the *Perthshire Courier*, November 9, 1854:

The late General Stuart, Count Roehenstart

It is very desirable that some one should bring forward authentic intelligence regarding the gentleman passing under that name, who died at Dunkeld on the 28th ult., in consequence of an injury by a fall from a stage-coach. A gentleman on whom we place reliance has known him as an occasional visitor of this country since the year 1830. He reports that the deceased General described himself as a son of the Duchess of Albany, the daughter of Prince Charles Stuart by Clementina Walkinshaw.

His father was also a Stuart, a Swedish count of Scottish descent, whom the Duchess had married without the sanction of her father. The Prince had become reconciled to the marriage, and the deceased remembered having often sat on the knee of his grandfather, at whose death, in 1788, he was about seven years old.

General Stuart had been in the Prussian [Russian?] service. He was a mild and amiable man, of dignified appearance and refined manners, and spoke of his connection with the Royal House of Stuart in modest and becoming terms. For many years he was accustomed to make a tour of the Highlands, to gratify his mind with recollections of the romantic struggle in which his grandfather had been engaged in 1745. He seemed to be an isolated individual, although in easy circumstances.

Assuming this report of his parentage and history to be correct, it is certainly an affecting consideration that the amiable old man should have perished in the Scottish Highlands in so unfortunate a manner. It may be added that, according to his own account, the title he bore was from an estate in Sweden, which had acquired from its first Scottish possessor the name of Roehenstart, with reference to a family legend, to the effect that at a hunt in the company of an early Scottish king, his ancestor had caused a *roe* and a *hen* to *start* at the same moment, greatly to the admiration of his Majesty.

This account is meant merely as a summary of what General Stuart stated regarding himself, and its verification by other intelligence is, of course, required before any great consequence can be attached to it.

Verification by further intelligence is, a bit more than a century after Roehenstart's death, furnished in part by this publication of his personal papers. With regard to the *roe*, *hen*, and *start*, as well as other matters, further intelligence is desirable.

CHAPTER ELEVEN

A Note on Finances

One can hardly follow the pleasantly roving life of Roehenstart without asking, How did he do it? What did he live on? Or, in the good American idiom, What did he do for a living? The frank answer is that we do not much know the source of his income: he seems seldom to have bothered about the problem of earning. At first one is inclined to suspect that he lived in a good period in which to live by one's wits—the period extending from the time when Richard Brinsley Sheridan so cleverly manipulated his creditors to the time of *Vanity Fair*. Roehenstart certainly had the charm necessary for living by his wits or off his friends. But he lived modestly and quietly: he was no frequenter of Vanity Fair. We find him often seeking small loans, but he always repaid them—though at times with exasperating tardiness. His life never appears as physically uncomfortable. He lived in good parts of the cities visited, and he traveled much. In London at one time he is found paying two guineas a week for lodgings, with *les vivres* supplied at additional expense. In Berne, Switzerland, he knew and possibly lived in a pension at six guineas a week—though he was proud of finding good cheap dinners elsewhere.

At the risk of tedious repetition it may be well to assemble the relatively few statements about his finances that are preserved to us: some of them are clearly untrustworthy and others hypothetical. There is of course the bare possibility of his being well connected through one or more married sisters. At the end of 1833 he wrote to his wife saying of a friend, "Count Alexander Potocki lost 25 millions landed property," and he adds, "the sister's daughter [Potocki's niece] nearly 40 married to one of my people Mr. Bower—about £2,000 a year." Such remarks probably indicate nothing as to Roehenstart's own income.

After he was beyond strong compulsion to fabricate (though the habit persisted) he said in 1839, "By the death of my father I came early into possession of a good estate besides a very large sum of ready money, the produce of my mother's diamonds." Since he certainly never got his mother's diamonds, one may be inclined to doubt also the statement about an estate from his father. It is probably his fictitious Swedish father of whom he intended one to think, whereas most likely he did get something from his actual Rohan father. Prince Ferdinand and Roehenstart evidently did on occasion use the same London bankers, Turnbull, Forbes and Company, and thus one may assume that Roehenstart got something from his real father.

In building up in his Memorial (1816) a picture of extreme indigence, Roehenstart exaggerated his poverty, for after the failure of the Memorial, he is doleful over the fact that from a "large sum of money owed to him in Russia" and from Fr. 60,000 due him in Paris (from the estate of his deceased father?) he could not at the moment raise "one shilling." This concealed background of his indigence may again be the product of imagination; but clearly throughout his career there was a small fortune or at least a small steady income always to be counted on.

While he was in Russia, he had money invested with one Sofniew, who late in 1811 proved completely bankrupt. That failure gave color to the story used to explain Roehenstart's hasty departure from Russia. He still left money behind him there, and at various times called upon Russian agents for money. He repeatedly asked the Duchess of Württemberg to forward sums due him—sometimes without result.

At the end of 1811 when he reached London, as he tells it in the Memorial, "I received news that a merchant, Mr. Forbes, in whose hands was placed the greatest part of my fortune had become bankrupt, and gone to the United States of America." Since this bankruptcy had taken place in 1802–3, Roehenstart probably knew of it before his arrival in London. Possibly the failure of Sofniew led Roehenstart to pursue to America the absent partner of the bankrupt firm of Turnbull, Forbes and Company. This firm, it will be remembered, had acted as agents for the Rohans in managing their estate in San Domingo. As a conclusion to the Forbes story Roehenstart added, 'After my arrival in Philadelphia I had the satisfaction to recover a part of my money." If months later he had anything like $18,000 to invest in his brig "Alexander," he probably secured the money either from Forbes or from the San Domingo estate. In spite of his failure to settle his small American debts before leaving, he probably left America with some money recovered from his cargo. He sailed from Salem with suspicious promptness after reaching a settlement.

He returned from America owing money to various friends, and he thought he paid them by sending to Mrs. Chapus a draft on Henry Cruger of Baltimore, drawn by Rev. John Audain, Rector of Charmouth, who to cover the sum had received £225 from Roehenstart. In the Memorial Roehenstart blows up this sum to £600 and complains bitterly of being cheated, though in this document he does not name Audain. It was the worthlessness of Audain's draft that involved Roehenstart with Count Sampigny, to whom the greater part of the money should have gone.

After the failure of the Memorial, it will be remembered that Roehenstart considered studying medicine: he wanted to earn a living. If his preserved papers show anything, they show that he had a passion for organizing and imparting information. He knew that his familiarity with various languages equipped him to be a teacher of languages. He did teach some young friends, but it is not clear that, after leaving his pupils in Russia, he was ever paid as a teacher of languages. He did, however, in 1818–19 escort two young gentlemen about Greece, Asia Minor, and the Greek islands, and evidently thought he should, for his services, receive something like Fr. 2,800. There was some trouble over the payment, with unknown results. In 1831–35 he was attached somehow to the staff of Admiral Sir Henry Hotham or some other officer, and was enabled to see the world of the eastern Mediterranean through the courtesy of the British Navy. Unless he had rank as an officer (which seems doubtful), the summer voyages on the "St. Vincent" and other ships would not be lucrative, but they probably involved no considerable expenditures on his part. Possibly he was paid as an interpreter or something of the sort. His naval career seems not to have lasted long. In 1839 he asked a friend to address him at "Baden, *Zum Zähringer Hof*, par Strasbourg," where, as he says, "I usually pass the summer": one must thus assume that his summer cruises with the navy were past. But whether he usually spent many summers in any one place may be doubted. He had few usual actions.

When really needed, money seems to have been available. Upon the failure of the Memorial, Roehenstart set off for France and Italy, with no talk of inability to raise "one shilling." In 1819 he told the French police (who certified his modest manner of life) that he lived only on advances made him by the banker Coutts and two other unnamed friends. The statement has to be accepted with some, but not complete, respect. Again, when his first wife died and was buried (1821) in London, he set off to Italy presumably to bear the unhappy news to her family in Turin or Milan. He left London on July 28, 1821, and was back again on August 15. The expenses of the hurried trip, as he set them down in detail, amounted to £206 6*s*. 10*d*.—a sum that belies indigence.

On one page that concerns money he notes that on June 1, 1823, he is to receive Fr. 6,211 40*c*. from the Duc de Castries. This is a particularly suggestive detail since in the Archives Nationales in Paris there exists a letter from Radesse (an agent) to Prince Ferdinand de Rohan, dated August 23, 1790, which reminds the Prince that "la terre d'Ollanville" is at the time in possession of the Duc de Castries, and cannot be used to raise funds. The duke of 1823 might still have the lands held by the duke of 1790 from the Rohans—a possibility that encourages one in the opinion that Roehenstart somehow did get property from his real father.

In an undated letter written on black-edged paper, presumably after the death of his second wife, Roehenstart sends money owed to his friend Colonel Julien with apologetic explanations as to the unhappy delays involved:

> Having a few days ago come into possession of a small inheritance, I feel a great pleasure in enclosing here £100 in two Fifty Pounds [*sic*] Notes, which, I trust, will arrive safely.—I deeply deplored my total incapacity, in spite of strong appearances, to repay my debt, when you did apply for it. Since that very long time I have tried earnestly to save money enough to refund a few Hundred Pounds; but after the bankruptcy of Hoffman & C° [1829] I gave up my plan as totally hopeless, for I was reduced to live upon an income which in the best years, did not exceed £140, and was sometimes under £100. I did then apply in vain to various persons who owed me, for money lent, more than ten times the amount of all my debts, and I took the resolution to ensure my life, and thus secure to my creditors at my death a sufficient sum to compensate them for having waited so long for their money. Still in the mean time I actually contrived to live in a respectable manner, although obliged by my rank and position to receive company and give now and then suiting entertainments. The thing was not easy; but I have accomplished it, paying regularly all my tradespeople, and never, ah never borrowing money, for I had suffered too much on this account.

One can hardly believe the whole of this statement. At least one may believe that Roehenstart lived modestly and respectably, and that he allowed debts to remain outstanding for a very long time. An examination of his papers leads one to doubt that he lived for long on less than £140 a year.

About the year 1825 Roehenstart had become interested in iron works at Terre Noire (near Lyons?) and invested in a forge there. The investment was unprofitable, but the mere fact of an investment indicates something in the way of initial income. A traveler must naturally in different places make use of different bankers. Roehenstart's bankers in various cities were frequently his surest addresses for letters. In 1823 Sampigny, unaware just where Roehenstart was, directed a letter to him in care of Messrs. Meulemeester & fils, bankers in Ghent, to be forwarded. In London Roehenstart used Coutts and Company and the new, powerful firm of N. M. Rothschild, whose representative in Naples (C. M. Rothschild) he also used. Before 1829 he had been presenting letters of credit from Herries Farquhar & Co. of London to Fridrich Christian Hoffman of Düsseldorf; but in 1829 Hoffman died, and his clients were then referred to M. Arnould Hasset of Düsseldorf. In 1823 Roehenstart had correspondence with an agent in Frankfurt-am-Main about the purchase of a lottery ticket, and in 1835 he received through M. S. Bing of Frankfurt an account of the sale of the "grand & magnifique palais, No. 70 a Vienne," from which Roehenstart was to profit. His connection with this sale is not known. He possessed more than one Russian bond, one of which he sold in 1831 for £300 2*s*. 4*d*.

It would not be strange if both of his marriages brought him modest sums. The expensive trip to Turin after the death of his first wife seems to indicate something of the sort, and evidently Mrs. Bouchier Smith, mother of the second wife, suspected a mercenary interest in her daughter on Roehenstart's part. Mrs. Stuart, as Constance was called after her marriage with Roehenstart, evidently did aid her husband financially. In one of his summaries of a letter to her (January 4, 1834) he says: "My way of thinking about money matters is different of [*sic*] most people &c. the money is *yours alone*, and if that which you seem to imply was the case, I should not ask for any to be forwarded to me: therefore I feel unkind the offer of £30 quarterly." She did, however, on occasion after the date of this letter send him money.

Probably he is quite right when he says that his way of looking at money differed from that of many people. He could keep very detailed accounts beautifully when necessary, but at other times he was annoyingly casual about money. At times he was capable of generosity. He preserved one or two begging letters and at least one very grateful letter thanking him for charity.

Six months before his death he was in Spain buying pictures—a proceeding that normally does not connote poverty. All that can be said is that somehow he managed to live the life of a not too impecunious gentleman, who still was normally at the moment short of cash. An accidentally incisive phrase in Roehenstart's obituary in the *Perthshire Courier*, November 9, 1854, sums up the matter as well as it can be stated: "He seemed to be an isolated individual, although in easy circumstances."

CHAPTER TWELVE

The Anatomy of Pretending

Varied and complicated are the processes of "pretending" to a position that is, because of irregular birth or out of sheer injustice, denied to the pretender. When the matter of birth is in question there are two distinct types of pretender: Type A realizes that in spite of illegitimacy he might expect generosity rather than severity of treatment; Type B is the clever impostor, who knows at heart that he has no claims, but brazenly pretends to a state to which, as he well knows, he has no rights. It is probable that the so-called "Sobieski Stuarts" belonged to this latter class. Roehenstart is not quite true to either type. It seems altogether sure that he honestly and rightly believed himself to be the grandson of Prince Charles Edward, and the son of the Duchess of Albany. Pretending began when he thought of his father. To gain a partial recognition it was hardly necessary in 1816 to insist on legitimacy, but since he could hardly acknowledge an archbishop as father, he might as well fabricate a respectable and wedded father for himself —and there the complications in pretending began. It is likely that some of the fabrication was done for him in his infancy; but it would be like him to add the wedding of his parents.

Roehenstart had a mind preconditioned in many obvious ways. There was nothing flamboyant about him. In part this might be due to his awareness of the scandal involved in his paternity. In any case he did not go about with royal insignia displayed before him—as did the Sobieski Stuarts. They chose the heroic Ossianic tradition in which to publicize their claims. Roehenstart was in the quiet, sentimental, self-pitying tradition of his time. He was no Harry Richmond. His early training, about which we know little or nothing, stimulated a love of books and especially of poetry and travel books. Even in his later travels Roehenstart enjoyed depicting the tenderer human aspects of the strange people whom he visited. Idyllic shepherds, fervid Greek patriots, charming housewives, hospitable Turks—not to mention dogs, camels, gazelles, and Arabian steeds—evoked his sympathies. Even in the slave trade as practised by the Turks he found humane and not unattractive aspects.

His taste in books followed also the vein of sentiment. Probably Rousseau was a dominant formative influence, and although Roehenstart thought he outgrew Rousseau, one may have doubts. Probably some of the French verses copied in his manuscripts were of his own composition: they are practically always tender. He knew English poetry well, including Shakespeare, and the more recent writers such as Pope, Gray, and others of the eighteenth century. Among more recent poets he was fond of Falconer's *Shipwreck*. And he was of course most affected by Lord Byron. Scott's more heroic romance gets less attention from him than Byron. He knew the French poets of his own time, and was familiar with Haller, Goethe, and Schiller, as well as the more famous poets of Italy. It was the emotional warmth and wisdom of these writers that chiefly aroused his interest: trumpet calls found faint echoes in his soul.

Literature and travel were avenues of escape, were in a sense refuges. A shy pretender is likely to be an aloof, isolated person. Roehenstart was by nature such: he had, so far as his papers show, no friends who continued throughout his adult life. He dreaded that men did not believe his story, and so he passed from one to another and another listener, and from one to another geographical environment. He traveled much in books, and confused his actual wanderings with wishful journeys made in books. A lack of fixed center toward which he might strive diversified his intellectual life. His real gift very likely was for languages. Ability to speak several languages enormously stimulates one's opinion of himself, and Roehenstart was proud of his abilities of that sort. He was tremendously interested in historical problems of human relations. Born a few years later he might well have achieved some reputation as a classical archeologist; but his mind rapidly involved itself warmly in any present problem—in military tactics, in chemistry, medicine, methods of smelting iron or building bridges, etc. But behind these diverse enthusiasms was the inhibiting fact of his royal blood. Men of his sort could not enter either learned professions or lucrative employments. On the other hand, it is probable that some psychological quirk about his birth kept him from marrying and settling at the Russian court. His departure from Russia was probably the great mistake in his career.

There was in his nature a strongly marked element of naïveté. One sees it, not pleasantly, in his attempt more than once to persuade a friend to transmit to other friends abusive letters (after reading them). One sees it in many places: for example, his thought that the priest who attended his mother at the time of her death might reveal details of her final confession. (Of course, Roehenstart at times was shrewd, and in this case he may simply have wished to present himself to Father Connolly, saying, "I am the son of the Duchess of Albany, whom she told you about"—and then await reactions.)

One might expect that his life at the Russian court would have modified this naïveté, although, after all, the Czar Alexander had his own store of this quality. It is possible, for example, that as chamberlain to the brother of the dowager Czarina, Roehenstart might have had a ready access to the highest personages: it is at least probable that he did not realize at all any lack of such access. And so in 1816 when he wished to present his Memorial to the Prince Regent privately and personally, he was grieved and simply astonished at the impossibility of securing such an audience. He assumes naïvely, later, that the Countess Norton as lady in waiting to his mother would be sitting by her deathbed listening to secret last words. Part of this is of course wishful thinking, but much of it is naïveté.

Roehenstart was, of course, unaware of this aspect of his mind. A sentimentalist is likely to think himself a person of subtle nuances of perception and appreciation—and not altogether without reason when it comes to casual contacts. But Roehenstart is more than a little complacent when he apologizes to his wife Constance: "If sometimes I have shown moments of impatience at seeing you could not understand what I felt, it was very wrong of me" [December 21, 1833]. The sentimentalist is almost sure to find the rest of the world at least a trifle obtuse; it is unfortunate when one states that finding to the world—or to one's wife.

Paradoxically, the sentimentalist believes that his own tender feelings and habits are common to all right-thinking men, and so he plies pathos excessively in his endeavors to secure "reclamations" from such men. Thus Roehenstart overplayed his poverty in his Memorial, and he doubtless overplayed it when he told his captive listeners the story of his wrongs. He should have realized that pathos is not very useful in the attempt to convince the inquisitive listener. It is no weapon at all in the face of suspicion. Frequently, doubtless, one listened to his sad story, and—after affording brief comfort—turned away. At times his personal charm made evidence unnecessary; and having no documentary proofs of his claims, Roehenstart had to rely on charm. Again, this is easy for one who believes that we are all made of the same sensitive clay and that the spark that kindles sympathy in one man will kindle it in another. This somewhat extreme notion is reinforced by such an outmoded idea as that royal blood speaks by instinct. Roehenstart was a strong believer in the power of "two words" spoken by one person of royal blood to move another such personage. The "sacred person" of the Prince Regent, so Roehenstart firmly believed, would recognize instantly the justice of Roehenstart's claims either at sight or at the sound of two words. So also, he thought, the Countess Norton, if he could have seen her, would have been won instantly to his cause. Charm and instinct are great matters when evidence is lacking.

They worked surprisingly on occasion. The young man from Stirling who briefly lodged in the same house with Roehenstart in Edinburgh was easily captivated. In general people seemed to recognize Roehenstart as unusual. Whenever anyone looked upon him approvingly at first sight, he was delighted. By implication—such cases seldom get on the record—when people were not impressed, they showed their limited perceptiveness. A typical triumphant moment is recorded when, as Roehenstart was leaving the house of Eki Effendi at Smyrna, the alluringly handsome black-bearded stranger, who had been silent during the visit and had "sat at his pipe unmoved," interrupted to say, as Roehenstart records it, "that he knew I was a gentleman of consequence from my manner." Such recognition is ambrosia to any pretender.

Doubtless an air of distinction, possibly inherited from his Rohan father, frequently graced Roehenstart, but more marked would be a related air of aloofness. Confidence came only in flashes; but isolation—complete as that of any picaresque hero—seemed a constant trait. Circles of friends came successively, but without any permanent accretion. Roehenstart is at home with shepherds as with courtiers: he can be sociable; but his aloofness was generally recognized, and is most striking. It is seen in his travel diaries, in which companions seldom appear. The account of the Sultan's review of the Russians is unusual, but even here the number and names of companions are not given. His accounts of roaming about the Troad, seemingly alone, his failure to mention fellow officers on the "St. Vincent," even when they must have shared in the entertaining of Smyrneot visitors—such silences about companions are typical and strange. Even more strange is the silence, in the papers preserved to us, concerning the foster parents who befriended him as a child, and the one single mention of a sister. Somehow—possibly because of his applications concerning his mother's fortune—he had cut himself off from any early friends. From among them only the Duchess of Württemberg survives in later mentions, and in this case the Duchess seems to have done the casting off: she fails to send him the money he claims as his own.

Aloofness was probably due less to delusions of grandeur than to lack of confidence. Roehenstart conceived himself less as a man born to rule or to live in marble halls surrounded by vassals than he did as a man of great moral integrity—a form of pretending to which many of us fall victim. In view of his early connection with Munich and with a Protestant point of view, it may be wise to quote the draft of a late letter of his, written in English to the pastor of an English congregation in Munich, whose mother had indulged in unjust accusations concerning a lady (Mrs. B?) to whom Roehenstart had long been a friend:

Dear Sir,—I feel called upon as a Member of your Congregation, as a man of honor, a Nobleman and a Gentleman, to address to you a few lines respecting the insinuations contained in Mrs. de C's letter to Mrs. B.—

In a few days we shall meet in the House of Him who sees into all our hearts, and I, here as in his presence, assure you that whatever may be the purport, or meaning of Mrs. de C's expressions, there is not one amongst those assembled there who can present herself at the Altar of our Heavenly Father with a conscience more void of offence towards Him, and more truly worthy of the respect of all mankind, than she to whom I am, and have been for several years as a Brother and protector, under Family misfortunes and difficulties which it would be as little proper as convenient to make public.

At our respective ages, we neither seek nor desire society, nor regret on that account the change of fortune which makes prudent a life of retirement, and I must say, it appears somewhat cruel that one so unobtrusive should have been troubled by such a letter as that of Mrs. de C.—

In conclusion allow me, as an older man than yourself, and one who has lived long in what is called "the world" to advise you to do, as I have done towards yourself, during my residence in Munich, to repulse with indignation reports which are derogatory to the good name of a fellow creature.

I am, Dear Sir,

Yours truly

Stuart

Munich

December 16th

Written in after the letter, in Roehenstart's hand, is the following comment:

> In answer to this letter Mr. de C, instead of coming himself or writing, immediately sent his mother to make an apology, and enquire what were the reports in circulation against him!—I replied it was impossible for me to mention them to any but himself; but I was quite willing to give him all the information he could require.
>
> The man has not dared to meet me!!

The high noble tone here taken contrasts sharply with the less pleasant aspect of pretending, which is the necessary element of deception: to put it bluntly, of *lying*. There can be no doubt that Roehenstart lied beyond the call either of duty or diplomacy. His invention of a respectable Swedish father for himself is forgivable, if needlessly elaborated in its details. In blackening the character of the Cardinal-Duke of York, he is probably following the slanders that his grandmother had taught him, but he should have been content to make the Cardinal "the enemy" who had deprived Charlotte Stuart's family of their rightful fortune, and not to have made him a murderer. Again when he says that the Cardinal and the Countess Norton on their respective deathbeds called for him repeatedly, he is deviously using the lies to draw out from others what he is sure is truth. When he pretends to recall sitting as a small child on the knee of his grandfather, Prince Charles Edward, he prevaricates amusingly.

In all pretending there is involved The Lie: that is inevitable. But one must differentiate between that to which Roehenstart pretended and that to which he laid no claim. He believed, and it was not difficult to believe, that Cardinal York had suppressed the true last will of the Duchess of Albany and thus deprived him of a fortune. He may actually have believed that his grandmother was truly married to Prince Charles (much as the Prince Regent was married to Mrs. Fitzherbert) but he pretended disingenuously that the Duchess of Albany was secretly married to a Swedish count, and that their son had been recognized by the royal grandfather. But he did not seriously ever claim, as (if one accepted his story) he might have claimed, not too firmly, to be a formal pretender to the British throne. His real rights, as he said more than once, extended only to Frascati, i.e., to his mother's fortune. He evidently thought the story of the Swedish count advisable for popular consumption, but he knew that his real father might be easily discovered. It must have been awkward when one pressed for an explanation of the origin of the name Roehenstart. Was it not a combination of *Rohan* and *Stuart*? And if so, the reason would be obvious. It was the scandal of that possible discovery that limited Roehenstart in his pretending to his mother's estate. Awareness of that possible discovery alone can explain Roehenstart's repeated talk of the "sad business" of his claims in his Memorial of 1816. There was nothing sad about the affair if his story was accepted. A mother born in wedlock as daughter to an exiled prince and married to a respectable Swedish nobleman is nothing to be apologetic about. Obviously an imaginative liar gets confused in the tangles of his own inventions.

After canvassing Roehenstart's career one is led to conclude that it was for him a very sad day, that on which as a child (?) he learned of his royal connections. When he was not pretending, he was an amiable, intelligent, and happy man; when pretending he was unhappy because the whole world seemed unjustly all against him. Even so he seems to have taken it largely without tincture of misanthropy. Melancholy he felt, and rather enjoyed; but that was as much the tone of his age as of his personal career. When the words SIC TRANSIT GLORIA MUNDI were placed on Roehenstart's tomb at Dunkeld, his friends merely meant to say, "Here lies the last of a once glorious house." Roehenstart ought not to be called the "fag-end" of a dynasty: in no fashion for which he was responsible, except his lying, was he a discredit either in manners or in intelligence to the house from which he claimed descent. It may even be true that much of his character as well as something of his personal appearance came from his Scottish grandmother, Clementine Walkinshaw. His life was quietly active and much of the time was happy. Yet there was little of the *gloria mundi* either in his tastes or in his behavior.

APPENDIX I

"*The Case of X against Y*"

[This document, in Roehenstart's hand, was drawn up ostensibly so that he might have legal advice about going to law in order to recover his papers. As he drew the document he used the following cipher in order to conceal the names of persons involved:

X is Roehenstart
Y is the second Mrs. Coutts, widow of Thomas Coutts

A is Prince Charles Edward
B is Clementine Walkinshaw
C is Charlotte, Duchess of Albany
D is Roehenstart's fictitious Protestant father
E is Thomas Coutts, the banker

To facilitate reading the names have been inserted in place of these initials.]

In the following hasty sketch of a very intricate Case, it is necessary to enter into some previous explanation to convey, if possible, a full idea of the nature of the claim which Roehenstart has against Mrs. Coutts, and which he proposes to bring before a Court of Law.

Prince Charles Edward, a Roman Catholic of exalted rank, married Clementine Walkinshaw, who on this account changed her religion. There was issue a daughter Charlotte, who has been generally thought to be illegitimate, because the marriage of her parents was kept secret. No one took the trouble of contradicting this report, but she inherited her father's property, in spite of the artful designs of her paternal Uncle, who wanted to appropriate it to himself: —this circumstance and the Register of the marriage of Prince Charles and Clementine give the most decided denial to the erroneous supposition respecting the validity of the marriage, and settle the question at once.

It is also necessary to state that from the very peculiar and extraordinary situation of all the parties, the history of this family has been shrouded by a thick veil, which circumstances rendered imperious. This explains the cause of that mystery and reserve with which Roehenstart has always spoken on this subject, when obliged unwillingly to allude to it.

Charlotte was married to Roehenstart senior:—they had a son Charles, who was to be brought up in the Roman Catholic Religion; but at the death of Prince Charles, Roehenstart senior, who was a Protestant, immediately changed the plan, which, he had been compelled to adopt, in compliance with the wishes of his wife's family, and caused his son to be instructed in the Protestant Religion, which he has always professed. This sudden change incensed Clementine, and a total rupture between them was the consequence.

Clementine, who was residing on the continent at the time of the war which sprung up from the French Revolution, forwarded to Thomas Coutts, her private friend, in London, a Tin Box containing papers of the utmost importance to Roehenstart.

Clementine died at Fribourg, in Switzerland, when Roehenstart was in the Russian Army, and which of course prevented his going to a Country which was then under the control of France; but directly after the peace he hurried to Fribourg, and claimed and received from her Executor, the property &c &c left by Clementine.

He then came over to England and saw Coutts, who was a Gentleman of great fortune, and had married a second wife.

Roehenstart was kindly received, and was in the habit of visiting and dining with them frequently. He made application to Coutts for the recovery of the Tin Box, the contents of which were of such great importance to him.

Coutts at first denied that he had ever received such a deposit, but Roehenstart brought to his recollection some circumstances referring to it, and shewed him besides a paper which mentioned that it had been forwarded to England to his care by Clementine.

Coutts then said that he had some confused idea that he had in fact received it, but he could not tell what had become of it.

Roehenstart explained his anxiety to one of Coutts's daughters, by his first marriage, who had been intimate with Clementine, and who was living at Coutts's house with her three daughters:—he told her in what an unfortunate situation he was placed by the loss of those papers, and how earnestly he wished to recover them.

Those four Ladies most kindly undertook to search for the Box amongst a great quantity of chests and trunks in the upper rooms of the house, and Roehenstart assisted them.

Mrs. Coutts went at the same time to the other house in Town, where Mr. Coutts's large concern was carried on, and she had the goodness to say to Roehenstart that she would make the strictest research in order to satisfy him.

At length Mrs. Coutts said the Box had been found in *the latter house*, and she appointed one of her husband's Clerks to look over a parcel of papers in conjunction with Roehenstart.

But Roehenstart most solemnly declares that the Box was not produced or shown to him. The only thing he saw was the before mentioned parcel of papers, and which were said by Mrs. Coutts to have been extracted from the Tin Box in question.

Unfortunately for him, those papers proved to be insignificant letters relating to various correspondences, but nothing was found which could in the least serve or interest Roehenstart.

Coutts is since dead, and his widow enjoys his fortune.—The widow who formerly had been all kindness to Roehenstart at once changed her manners towards him, without his having given her the slightest cause, and behaved even with rudeness to him, consequently he has not, for a long time, seen her, or any of the other members of the Family.

Roehenstart now confidently states that those papers which he claimed from Coutts were not only of the utmost importance to him, but would have been the means of his actually recovering various large sums of money &c. which had been reserved by Prince Charles Edward as a separate provision for him, and sent to that effect to the charge of his Grandmother, Clementine.

The sealed up Tin Box containing them, *which was at first denied*, *Roehenstart has never seen*, *altho' some of its contents were shown to him*.

Roehenstart is unwilling to draw an uncharitable inference, but justice obliges him to do so, well knowing that Coutts raised himself to great wealth partly through the means of Roehenstart's Grand father [Prince Charles].

Roehenstart is desirous of ascertaining whether measures can not be adopted to compel Mrs. Coutts to make him some indemnification for the great injury, and severe pecuniary loss he has sustained from having been deprived of these valuable documents, and he is confident that Mr. Coutts's wife and her three daughters, would all acknowledge that their father said in their presence, *that he had* received the Box, which declaration, with Roehenstart's entreaties, induced them to occupy two whole days in searching for it.

APPENDIX II

Summaries of Letters to Mrs. Stuart

[These jottings are given in the order in which they occur on a folded correspondence sheet. The handwriting is very small and at times difficult. All dates or phrases in brackets are editorial additions to what Roehenstart wrote.]

[1830?] Letter of the 5th August—Baumcleff—Capt. Steel with his brother —gracious reception

21st things going on very well—intended journey to Dresden after the season—2 months longer—La Grippe—dancing 8 hours for a cure—intended present copy of a pretty picture & music, clock, disque magique—soup ladle

18 7bre [1830 or 1831] Baden—2 persons from Paris—"hesiter à lui cracher au visage de peur" etc. Going in another direction—to Naples for the winter —direct to C. M. deRothschild the banker at Naples, etc. forwarding the box from Strasbourg

NAPLES S^{a} LUCIA No. 21—7th Nov^{ber} 1833—arrived last night & lose no time in writing &c. great neglect in the various post offices—The Carlo Alberti seazed at Marseille, obliged to disembark &c. great annoyances on the road, endless vexations—Consuls, Customs officers policemen, all pack of thieves—paid to that of Marseille 8f 45—the rascal! to send in January £40 if it suits —wretched copy of the portrait much criticised at Baden—Received the letter 17 days on the road.

3^{d} Dec^{ber} 1833. direct poste restante Castellamare expedient & necessary to write again.—not much pleased with my position here—I have to deal with a most unfeeling heartless person, proud in the extreme degree, capricious & revengeful for supposed & imaginary wrongs.—said I might go to law if I chose. I foretold an eruption 10 days before it took place & to the precise hour &c. the Count Alex.^{der} Potocki lost 25 millions landed property—the sister's daughter nearly 40 married to one of my people Mr Bower—about £2000 a year—directions to be paid in Ducats my pretty cane stolen &c

Castellamare 20.th Dec.^{ber} 1833—most uneasy at not hearing from you &c. returning to Town which I must regret &c delightful spot, classical recollections & learning returning by degree into my thick head—I walk the silent streets An animated description of Pompeii went to see the eruption which they call mine & the horse fell, the rain broke & I jumped out and rolled in the dust with a slight contusion & very narrow escape—the horse was killed on the spot having two legs broken and the poor man died on the following morning! —Saturday the 21st Dec.^{ber}

Bagnibaldi Largo del Castello n.º 20—Jany the 4th 1834

The idea that you think I have been unkind is distressing to me & I receive in this moment y^{r} letter of the 23^{d} Nov.^{ber} after a vast deal of trouble to recover it.—I lament you should allow y^{r} spirits to be so depressed: it is most unreasonable to say you are forgotten by the whole world, no indeed, my dear, you are my best, my only friend, and if sometimes I have shown moments of impatience at seeing that you could not understand what I felt, it was very wrong of me &c—the annoyance about Coutts I might have easily borne longer &c my way of thinking about money matters is different of most people &c—the money is *yours alone*, and if that which you seem to imply was the case, I should not ask for any to be forwarded to me: therefore I feel unkind the offer of £30 quarterly.—I am far from being emersed in pleasures & gaieties as you fancy &c—I have found it more convenient since our return to Town to live by myself—so I am here alone on Christmas I endeavoured to be cheerful & it was within a few days the anniversary of a melancholy loss &c She was more capricious & peevish than usual, so that the day ended by some unpleasant words. We shall have, I hope, a merry Christmas this year &c but to avoid deserving the reproach of concealment I trust it will not be at Ab[béville] which I hate.

Naples Tuesday 28 Jany 1834—Rec^{d} Saturday the 2 letters, that by the Banker 2 hours before &c 'tis vexatious to have written to R. he is a grasping Jew, a fool &c—I share in no gaieties of the place—sometimes in my aunt's Box, but the annoyance of strict toilet &c—She is tired & speaks of going to Rome for the holy week, but unless she acts with justice towards me I shall not allow myself to be coaxed to accompany her—a great beauty who forgets she is no longer young—her woman & major domo enraged and opposing my ascendancy &c she has a bad heart and is the counterpart of the C. of Albany—genuine account of the fall, quite over in its effect—presence of mind in danger—&c. Leaving Naples without regret—the coquet at Ab[béville]—try to part with the house in Geo. S^{t} to Mr H. You had money enough to take £25 to buy the Piano Forte &c When I think of the uncertainty of any proceedings depending on the whim of a capricious woman &c—direct after 25 Feby to Marseille poste restante—intending to go there by the Steam Boat—I certainly do not like Ab. but I cannot account for the feeling of sadness I experience at the idea of returning to it, although at the same time my heart is filled with joy by the prospect of being reunited to you. I am far, I think, from being superstitious, I never was so, but sinister forbodings, which I oppose in vain, tell me that something very unpleasant is to happen there &c—I never liked residing in France—prefer even England If you would but consent to my selecting some pretty spot in Switzerland &c the house and furniture easily disposed of—and the young Lady a gainer by the change—occupy myself with agriculture &c I have no other desire but that of pleasing you, in fact I wish to be very good—you have numerous items to answer—

2 March MARSEILLE. Fine passage of 5 days—defer entering into any detail until our meeting—letters having been opened—setting off by Montpellier wishing to see the man who has got the chief part of the Countess of Albany's fortune—passed a day with Count Castellane and the Duke of Harcourt

STUTTGART 25 July 34 the lusty Gent.^{n} with me in the mail Lt Gal de Péré —arrived on M.^{dy} at 1 o'clock, at 1/2 past two at Kehl. thunder storm—a wind mill in a blaze. brother off.^{er} p.^{ce} Hohenlohe

DRESDEN 26 Aug.st accident of one fore wheel going off—1 two legs broken —1 an arm, the 3.^{d} senseless and spitting blood—myself much bruised and two wounds on the head—m.^{r} Peascu [?] not known at Carlsruhe.—

D.[resden?] 8th September change of plan, came here with the resolution of submitting to many unpleasant things &c but why should I relate &c told me she did not believe any longer what I said—a circumstance which would strike you with wonder—The Countess is going to Italy & proposed me to accompany her which I declined—her people have brought the heavy things I compelled them to leave behind at Florence she exulted in the communication &c—Consulted a celebrated Counsellor—he finds a flaw in the Deed of Sale—offer of the 4th part of the value.—promised this would be the last time I gave the choice to return immed.^{ly} to Paris & come again next summer or remain in Germ^{y} until a final decision. Bower—extravagant—Galig.^{s} article The Countess going I do not wish to remain at Dresden—she countenanced me &c.

APPENDIX III

The Battle of Saalfeld (1806) *Reported by an Eyewitness*

[In October 1806 the ducal family of Saxe-Coburg, hoping to avoid the troops of Napoleon, removed from Coburg to Saalfeld. It was an unlucky move; for although there was no battle at Coburg (which, however, the French occupied), from the château of Saalfeld the terrified family had to witness the bloody combat of October 20. A story of this battle as seen from the château is preserved among the papers of Charles Edward Stuart, Count Roehenstart. The manuscript is in the fine small handwriting of Roehenstart himself, though he is probably not the author. He was, to be sure, at Coburg in 1806 or early 1807 and from there he went to St. Petersburg, to assume the office of chamberlain to the Duke of Württemberg, generalissimo in the Russian armies. Antoinette, the Duchess of Württemberg, was a daughter of Francis, Duke of Saxe-Coburg. The author of the story here presented was apparently the unidentified daughter of a Prussian general. She may have been only temporarily with the Saxe-Coburg family, but she seems an intimate in their group. One may theorize that she sent this "Souvenir de Saalfeld" to Russia, where Roehenstart transcribed it; but the early history of the document is hypothetical. It certainly is a manuscript practically contemporary with the events depicted. It is written in French, which is here translated. In the following list of persons mentioned in the story those most important are signalized by an asterisk:

The Family

*Francis, reigning but ailing Duke of Saxe-Coburg (1750–Dec., 1806).
*Augusta Sophia of Reuss-Ebersdorff, Duchess of Saxe-Coburg[1].

[1] The Duchess, in her diary (edited by H.R.H. the Princess Beatrice, *In Napoleonic Days* (1941), pp. 1–10) gives a similar account of this battle.

*Princess Caroline Reuss, niece of the Duchess.

Ernest, "prince hereditary," who succeeded Duke Francis, his father. He left Saalfeld to fight with the Prussians.

*Princess Sophia Frederica, daughter of Duke Francis and wife of Count Mensdorff.

*Emanuel, Count of Mensdorff-Pouilly.

Princess Juliana, youngest daughter of Duke Francis, separated from her husband, Grand Duke Constantine of Russia. She "emigrated" from Coburg shortly before the story begins.

Mre de Coburg, presumably Field Marshal Frederick (b. 1757) who after 1794 lived in retirement at Coburg.

Prince Leopold (1790–1865), youngest son of Duke Francis, and years later King of the Belgians.

The Governor of Prince Leopold (mentioned but unnamed).

Prussians mentioned

King William III.

*Prince Louis Ferdinand, killed in the battle.

General Mafling.

M. Harden.

*Amelie, author (?) of the story; sister of Mme Huelssen.

French officers present

Lannes, Marshal (Jean Lannes, duc de Montebello).

Augereau, Marshal (Pierre-Francois-Charles, duc de Castiglione).]

1 October 1806

We left Coburg at a terrible moment hoping in Saalfeld to avoid the horrors of war. I said good-bye to my sister Huelssen on her very birthday, oppressed with dark forebodings, not knowing when I might have the sweet pleasure of seeing her again. I got into the carriage with Madame the Duchess and her niece the Princess Reuss, and soon lost myself in darkest melancholy. A dreadful dream that I had had a fortnight before the departure of Madame the Grand Duchess haunted my memory.

In my dream I saw her depart, and shortly afterwards we followed. In passing through a small town and coming to a square like the courtyard at Saalfeld, we saw a military funeral march by—with doleful music. In vain I asked the occasion of this sad ceremony: no one could or would tell me the name and quality of the deceased. The sight made me weep bitterly, and when I awoke I was bathed in tears. The idea that this might presage the death of Monsignor the Duke, who had been long ailing, made me shiver. When I told this dream to some of the ladies of the court, they shared my disquiet, and in spite of my efforts to get rid of or to counteract the effect of the dream, I still had a very strong image of it, and upon our departure I was more affected than ever.

We reached Saalfeld at eight o'clock in the evening, and it was not without emotion that I saw the pleasing chateau, where in better days I had so agreeably passed a happy time.

The hereditary Prince arrived in the night with Monsieur Harden, eagerly preparing to go and join his friend the King of Prussia. The whole day passed sadly: painful forebodings disquieted the hearts of his parents, especially that of his sensitive mother. In the evening an adjutant arrived to announce the approach of Mafling's regiment; we had gay music during our supper, but far from enlivening us it only increased our solicitude, reminding us of the dangers that this dear Prince, about to depart, was to undergo.

On the two days following we watched Prussian regiments march by. The next day we had the pleasure of welcoming Princess Sophie, the Count her husband, and their charming infant six weeks old. She hadn't been able to join us sooner, and the pleasure of this reunion for the moment calmed our fears for the future—unaware that danger was so close at hand.

Thereafter every day we had Prussian officers at dinner. Many of them knew my father, whose bravery they praised; and especially the old General Mafling spoke of it with much kindness. I renewed my acquaintance with certain Prussian and Saxon officers from the *avant poste* of Prince Louis Ferdinand, and with pleasure heard them praise this brave fighter whom I had known from my tenderest years. He came often to see my father, whose friend he was since they had fought together. He was expected at Rudolstat two leagues from Saalfeld, and I had therefore some hope of seeing him again after having lacked that pleasure for eight years. I went back over those happy days, telling myself that on every occasion I was his little favorite. We talked about him for a long time, and I hoped soon to see him arrive on his way to battle and to victory.

That night by a courier from Coburg the Duchess was informed of the arrival there of the French—news that distressed us greatly, though we had foreseen that event. Mre de Coburg, *grand Ecuyer*, the same day received orders from the hereditary Prince to join him as soon as possible with his horses; and he without delay yielded to his wishes. Count Mensdorff had likewise the greatest desire to visit the King and his brother-in-law, who had suggested it; but happily for us our one remaining defender yielded to the entreaties of his wife, who was not at all willing to be separated from him.

The next day brought new perils. The French drew nearer, and in the evening we saw a quarter of a league away a small camp of Prussians, distinctly lighted, and further off there were troops advancing towards them, singing and carrying torches: it made indeed a fine effect. Very late we went back to the apartments of the Princess Reuss, from which we could see perfectly what was happening. We saw a great fire on the edge of the forest, which filled us with fright and a fear that certain villages had been fired or that the

French camp had been set up there. We went to bed in the keenest anxiety; later we learned that unfortunately it had too just a basis.

The tenth of October at seven in the morning the Princess Reuss awoke me, surprised at finding me asleep while the sound of muskets was noisy; but, having passed a very bad night, my sleep towards morning was so profound that nothing could disturb it. As soon as possible I joined their Highnesses at windows from which we could descry a small number of Prussians and Saxons drawn up for battle. Soon afterwards Count Mensdorff returned from a visit that he had paid to Prince Louis Ferdinand, whose joy at meeting his old friend had been great. He was at the head of his small detachment, and expected only a small engagement between advance guards. Unfortunately since he knew not at all the number of his enemies, he could not foresee the moment of attack. Far off I recognized this amiable Prince, distinguished by his noble bearing, his superb figure; and on seeing him my fears vanished: I thought his defeat impossible, for his appearance inspired confidence, and seemed to promise victory. Never, alas! was hope more cruelly deceived.

Where shall I find colors strong enough to paint the picture of these agonizing scenes? At eleven o'clock the battle began to look serious; one heard only the boom of cannon and the volleys of infantry. From out of the forest we saw the French advance: the first painful impression that I felt was caused by the arrival of some wounded, who were carried from the battle and passed under our windows. The bravery of this small troop, so few in number, gave me hope. The governor of Prince Leopold told us of having seen the artillery-men that morning on bended knees praying before their cannon—all prepared for death.

At noon we had a little dinner in a room on the other side of the chateau, where we were safe from bullets. That was not at all my fear: I should have preferred to remain at the window, but finally I tore myself from the sad spectacle, which still fascinated me, and sat down at table. No one could eat: Count Mensdorff rose from time to time to tell us what was happening. Soon he brought the sad news that the Prussians had lost the battle, and shortly the French would advance towards the chateau.—Oh, never shall I wipe from my memory those terrible words! We ran to the windows, from where we saw the retreat of the small body of Prussians and Saxons who had so valiantly fought against fifteen thousand French from six o'clock in the morning until two o'clock in the afternoon. We could still see in the distance a cavalry attack. My brave compatriots did their best; I admired their courage and would have given my life at that moment if it would have been of any use to them. Soon a portion of the victorious army came back; certain hussars of the 9th regiment entered the court of the chateau noisily, and before my eyes fired at an unlucky Prussian hussar who had taken refuge there. He defended himself a long time, and disappeared pursued by his enemies. They fired also at Coburg soldiers, and went into the guardhouse to see if any Prussians were hidden there. Having found nothing they quieted down. Count Mensdorff went down to remind them that the soldiers of Coburg were not their enemies. He gave them some wine, and they were content.

Poor Princess Sophie, seeing her husband descend was in despair: she feared for his life and ran to the cradle of her infant, to protect it in case its life were threatened. Her imagination was so inflamed that the danger seemed to her far greater than it actually was. Her husband came back and consoled her; our servants brought to the chateau certain Saxon officers, now captives, who were covered with wounds. They were given aid and were bandaged.

Soon a French adjutant came to announce the arrival of the Marshal Lannes and his officers, who were to lodge in the chateau. He ordered a supper for thirty persons. Princess Caroline Reuss and I were compelled to quit our apartments to make room for these gentry, and half an hour later the court was full of carriages, horses, and servants of the Marshal, who himself arrived immediately. He went to the apartment of Monsignor the Duke, and, while talking to him, in came an adjutant to remit the medals of Prince Louis Ferdinand, with the sad news of his death, met while fighting for his country, unwilling to submit to a shameful captivity. Count Mensdorff with tears in his eyes came to tell us this devastating news. We all wept for this unhappy prince, but no one felt so keenly as I: he was the friend of my father, and the honor and glory of the Prussian army who adored him.

That evening we spent in a dimly lighted room in a silence woeful and stupified; the feeble light of a single lamp perfectly suited the somber melancholy of our hearts. We were the more depressed by the cries of the poor inhabitants of Saalfeld, who, given over to pillage, came for refuge to the chateau, begging for aid against the excesses of the troops. Among others came an unfortunate old man of eighty years, led by his two daughters, to voice his bitter complaints: he had been robbed, and without respect for his white hairs or his body bent with the weight of years, he had been brutally beaten. Revolting spectacle that tore the tears from our eyes and made our hearts bleed! Princess Sophie offered him her chamber for refuge, and there he tasted some hours of repose. Mre de Mensdorff went to Marshal Lannes and gave him a picture of the excesses that his troops were allowing themselves, and the Marshal ordered a check to pillage and to the furors of the soldiers.

We had to go to bed without supper, for victuals were rare, and insufficient for all. It was the Duke alone who from his feeble health felt this privation.—I went to bed at last, my heart torn, thinking of the unfortunate prince and of my dear brothers, for whom the same fate was perhaps prepared. I sought sleep but did not the whole night find it.

The next day we had to witness a scene more painful than all those preceding. How shall I describe it?—Seated at my window, quite lost in reflection on the past, absorbed in grief and pain, I was roused by the Princess Reuss who had called my attention to note in the distance on the battlefield a stretcher on which was borne an unhappy wounded man. Suddenly we saw it surrounded by a group of soldiers who accompanied it to the sound of gay and victorious music: they came to the chateau and set it down in the middle of the court.—Great Heavens! what a scene! I recognized Prince Louis Ferdinand, that superb young man, the pride of the Prussian army, once brilliant as the day-star, now wan and pale in death.—I saw the nephew of the great Frederick pillaged, despoiled, covered only with some remnants of clothing—ah, never shall I forget that terrible sight!

Marshal Lannes and his officers watched the spectacle, and the Marshal asked Count Mensdorff, who approached the body of his friend and grasped the hand now lifeless, if this was the man whom he had known. The Count replied only, "Yes," fixing his tearful eyes on the adored prince, covered with wounds: he had talked with him on the very eve of his glorious death.

The men who had brought in the stretcher now wished to leave it there, but the Count suggested that it would be an honor for them to carry this valiant fighter to the church, and he himself led the funeral convoy of his friend.—I returned pale and downcast to the rooms of the Princess Sophie; both of us, overwhelmed with the same sorrow, bitterly bewailed this amiable prince.

Marshal Lannes left us that same day, and soon afterwards came an adjutant of Marshal Augereau to announce the Marshal's arrival that evening. He duly came at five o'clock with his staff, which was not so numerous as that of Marshal Lannes. After dining he paid a long visit to their Highnesses and conversed especially with Madame the Duchess concerning the results of this fighting—and unfortunately his predictions were only too well realized. These soldiers also began pillaging, but the Marshal soon stopped it. He had the further kindness before departure to give us a gendarme as protector who was a completely genteel man.

The day after this day of horror I was so affected that I had a fever and was obliged to stay in bed. The corpse of that unfortunate prince was forever in my mind as well as the thought of the danger run by my dear brothers. The kindness shown me on this occasion by Monsieur and Madame Mensdorff I shall never forget.

The thirteenth of October—the day fixed for our departure—I was a bit better, and the idea of paying the last honors to the hero who had fallen in battle restored my strength. Unknown to everyone I went to the church, accompanied by two servants and a basket full of flowers. On the way I passed many wounded, Prussians and Saxons, to whom I gave what bits of money I had with me, but always quickening my step to reach the church. I approached the coffin and helped place a crown of laurels on the beautiful brow of the prince, a crown that he well merited. His fine mouth seemed to smile on me; he was not yet disfigured by death: his features were still marked by nobility. In cutting a lock of his hair, which I shall always keep as a bitter but precious souvenir, I saw the mortal wounds that his bosom had received, and the scissors fell from my hand. Overwhelmed with grief I dropped to my knees before the coffin, entreating heaven fervently to watch over the days of my brothers. The solemn tolling of a bell suddenly struck my ear, and rising I saw a crowd of soldiers surrounding the coffin, who sorrowed for their prince. But what especially struck me was an aged French officer who wept profusely. The sight touched me; he looked sadly at me and said, "It is the fatality of one of my comrades that I lament." Much moved I cast a last look on him whom I shall lament all my days, and placed my handkerchief, wet with tears, over his wounds, and covered his coffin with flowers. I went back to the chateau heart-broken, agitated and anxious lest my action should be known, but content with having performed what I regarded as a duty on the part of a daughter of a Prussian general who had tenderly loved the deceased.

We left at once for Coburg at the risk of meeting on the roads all the supply trains of the corps of the French army; for the fear of being exposed to new scenes of war determined their Highnesses to set out with a passport from Marshal Augereau. As we went through the city we were pained to see a number of wounded in the streets and to hear the woeful cries of poor people desolate and despoiled of their meager possessions. Our road took us very near to the battlefield, and we saw many corpses that were not yet buried. At the sight I shivered and covered my eyes to shut out such scenes of horror. I let myself lapse into an actual state of stupidity.

We were accompanied by all the soldiers of Coburg who had been at Saalfeld, and we formed a large convoy. Most of the servants had to go afoot, since there were not enough horses. The pieces of baggage were carried by the cattle, whom we dared not outdistance in spite of their slowness. We stayed together since Count Mensdorff, who had the passport and was our advance guard dared not outdistance us. But he had much trouble keeping us all together. Since all the while carriages became separated, he had assigned six soldiers as escort for each vehicle. We were surrounded like prisoners. As we passed through the woods, across their shelters, their numbers seemed to multiply, and we gave the impression of being escorted by a large body of troops. Soon we met with a unit of French supply wagons. M. de Mensdorff talked to the officer, and showed him the passport. He at once ordered his people to make way for our vehicles as far as possible, and this first mix-up passed off very well.—In the villages we saw on all sides the spots where the French had pitched camp, and where, lacking straw, they simply spread out the wheat. Terror still stood in the faces of the poor peasants, and some with tears in their eyes showed us their burned houses. Our good Duke gave away all the money he had with him.

It was getting dark when we met the second (and larger) supply train: the road was so narrow that we could hardly pass. The French lighted bundles of straw and came so close to their wagons that we were afraid they might take fire. They complained much of the bad road, and swore incessantly. The many men and wagons that blocked the way, the shouting from all sides, stunned us. The torches that lightened the darkness let us see the rough faces of some Italians that were frightening. It all made an extraordinarily wild scene.

At last we reached Gräfenthal—but quite fatigued. Poor Princess Sophie was worried lest the journey make her infant ill, but the little blossom behaved beautifully, smiled at us as we entered the inn—and fell asleep at once. We also were early in bed. The hostess told us that two days before thirty French fighters had slept in straw in the same room. The idea was terrifying.

In the morning we could not set out before eight o'clock because of a terrible fog. It was the awful day of the battle of Jena, where everything worked for the defeat of the Prussians. Even nature seemed to hide the enemy, whose position was learned only too late. An overwhelming anguish seized me, especially when I thought that one moment or another might snatch away the lives of my dear brothers, though I was unaware that on that very day there would be a battle that one would remember all one's days.

We went by way of Judenbach where nine houses that had been burned still smoked and infected the air: everywhere we might see the distressing tracks of the enemy. At six in the evening we reached Coburg, where we were impatiently expected.

One seemed to awaken from a sad dream, and yet what we had seen was only a small beginning of the great misfortunes that were in store for the House of Prussia.

AMÉLIE

Index

Abbati, Contessa degli. *See* Norton, Maria, Countess
Albany, Louise, Countess of. *See* Stolberg, Louise von
Albestroff, Clementine, Countess of. *See* Walkinshaw, Clementine, Countess of Albestroff
Alewyn and Dirck, 75, 89, 90
Alexander I, 72
Alfieri, Vittorio, 2, 99
Alfort, Lord (John Graeme), 54
Allen, Charles Manning, 113
Ancienne Noblesse, Ordre d', 51, 84
Archives Nationales (Paris), vi
Assig, Augustus, 70, 72
Athens, 88, 92, 93
Audain, Rev. John, 38, 66, 120

B——, Mrs. (of Munich), 128
Bachaumont, Louis Petit de, 12
Bassano, Maret, Duke of, 48
Beale, B., 84
Beauclerk, Lady Amelius, 113, 115
Bedford, fifth Duke of, 8
Bethune-Charost, Comte de, 12
Bloomfield, General Benjamin, 65
Bodleian Library, v
Bologna, 10
Bordeaux, 11
Bower (Bauer ?), Mr., 118, 135
Bremont, Abbé, 43
Bretteville, General Lenormand de, 84, 85
British Museum, vi, 19
Brunnern family, 88, 92
Buissy, Mlle. de, 23
Bute, Lady (Frances Coutts, wife of the first Marquess of Bute), 47, 48
Byron, George Noel, Lord, 98

C——, Rev. Mr. (of Munich), 128
Cales, M., 84
Cambrai, Archbishop of. *See* Rohan-Guéméné, Ferdinand
Campbell, Lady Charlotte, 99
Canaris, Constantine, 96–97
Carnea, Barone di, 52
Caroline, Princess of Wales (wife of the Regent), 42, 70
Castallane, Count, 136
Castries, Duc de, 121
Cesarini, Ange, Bishop of Milievi, 39, 61
Chapus, Mrs. E., 36–38, 120
Charles Edward ("Charles III"), Count of Albany: alleged acknowledgment of Roehenstart, 110; with Clementine, 5–6, 53; legitimates Charlotte, 3; marries Louise, 2, 3, 55; old age, 5; reconciled to his brother, 7; wanderers after 1745, v, 1
Charlotte, Princess of Wales (daughter of the Regent), 73, 74
Chetwynd, Lord, 76
Clarke, Dr. (of Smyrna), 104
Clarke, J. S., 77
Coburg, Francis, Duke of, 23. *See* Saxe-Coburg family
Coleridge, E. H., 48
Constantin, Grand Duchess, 46
Couppey, P., 40, 41
Coutts, Harriot, 64
Coutts, Thomas: aids (?) Roehenstart financially, 120, 135; asked to buy a San Domingo estate, 12, 27; critical of Cardinal York, 58; kind to Clementine Walkinshaw, 9, 40; in Paris with his daughters, 9
Croix, De la, 22

D'Angles, Comte, 84
Darnley, Earl of, 77, 110
Dashkoff (Russian in Washington), 59
D'Entraigues, 84
Dirck. *See* Alewyn and Dirck
D'Oyley, General John Walpole, 116

Eki Effendi, 103, 104

Ellis, Daniel, 73
Enghien, Louis Antoine Condé, Duc d', 30
Ettenheim, 30
Evelina (of St. Petersburg), 24, 27

Fazackerley, Mr., 45
Ferdinand, Prince. *See* Rohan-Guéméné, Ferdinand
Ferguson-Teppers of Warsaw, 17
Fitzherbert, Mrs., 78, 129
Fladgate, Messrs., 80
Forbes, Lady Elizabeth, 42
Forbes, John (bankrupt), 27, 59, 119
Francis II, Emperor, 1

Galignani's Messenger, 109
George, Prince Regent (later George IV), 2, 61, 66, 70
George III, 74
Glasgow Chronicle, 82, 109 ff.
Gloucester, William Frederick, second Duke of, 49, 66, 85
Gonsalvi, Cardinal, 60
Gordon, Sir William C., 99
Gouppy of Paris (banker), 43
Graham's Island, 91
Griffith, Jules, 25
Guildford, Susan (Coutts), Countess of, 48

H——, General (in Russia), 24, 27
Haiti (Rohan estate), 30, 31
Haller (banker ?), 41
Hamilton, Mrs., of Kames Castle, 19, 20, 78, 109
Harcourt, Duke of, 136
Hardwicke manuscripts, 19, 69
Harrison, Charles, 113
Harvard College Library, iii, 6
Haswell, E. S., 70
Heather grave story, 16
Henry Benedict, Cardinal-Duke of York (called "Henry IX"), 56; attitude toward Charlotte, 6, 55; dealings with Clementine, 2, 58; death, 39; false charges against, 43, 54, 57, 60; letter to Pius VI, 6; will, 61
Herculès, Marquis (?), 84, 85
Hoffman & C., 121
Hohenlohe, Prince von, 49, 136
Hotham, Sir Henry, 97, 98, 120
Howard, Sophia, 56
Huelsen, Mme., 138
Hughes, Margaret, 115
Humboldt, Alexander von, 34

James Edward ("James III"), 1, 53
Jena, Battle of, 144
Johnson, "Countess". *See* Walkinshaw, Clementine
Julien, Colonel, 115, 121

Korff, A. M. (signature of Roehenstart), 17, 44
Korff von Schmissing, Count, 17
Kramer, H., 27

La Force prison, 70
Lamartine (poet), 98
Lambertini, Giula, Princess of, 10
Leinster, William Robert, 2d Duke, 8
Leopold of Saxe-Coburg, Prince (later King of the Belgians), 23, 66, 85, 140
Libau, letter written from, 28
Liége, 1, 11
Limbourg, Prince de, 84
Litchfield, N. C., 63
Löwenberg, R. de, 40
Louis XV, 54
Louis Ferdinand, Prince of Prussia, 23, 140 ff.
Ludlow, Edmund, 46

Macdonald, 51
Madison, James (President), 33
Maeri, Theresa ("Maid of Athens"), 98
Mahmoud, Sultan, 101–2
Maret, Duke of Bassano, 48
Marianne (of St. Petersburg), 24, 27
Messence, Comte de la Garde, 25, 34, 83
Meulemeester & fils, 122
Milnes, Keith, 19, 69
Montagu, Lady M. W., 100
Munich, 71 *et passim*
Murat, Joachim, 45
Murillo, 114

Napoleon I, 11, 21, 45
Nashe, H. F., 76
Neuwied, 80
New Times, 77
Norton, Maria, Countess, 39, 42–45

Oates, Mark, 20
Oban Times, 16
Osmond, Marquis d', 71

Pecchio, Count, 97
Perthshire Courier, 116
Petrettini, Countess (of Corfu), 52, 65

Phoenician remains, 34, 60
Pius VI, 6, 47
Pius VII, 45
Port au Prince (Rohan estate), 12
Potocki, Count Alexander, 118, 135
Purdy, Mr. and Mrs. (of Smyrna), 104
Pyrmont in Waldeck, 12

Roehenstart, Auguste Maximilien, Count (fictitious parent), v, 48, 56, 57, 71
Roehenstart, Charles Edward Stuart, Count (and Baron Korff)
in America: blockade-running project, 32 ff., 59–60; "pretensions," 39; reasons for going, 31, 59; return to England, 38, 60; as told to Messance, 34; travels, 31
behavior as pretender: awarded Ordre d'Ancienne Nobless, 51; claims against Mrs. Coutts, 131–33; comment on the death of Charlotte, Princess of Wales, 73–74; comment on the "Stuart papers", 77; early ancestry (alleged), 77, 110; letter in the *Sunday Review*, 31; refrains from talking of his claims, 113; watches news about Royal Stuarts, 77
biographical data: history of his papers, v, 116; lack of documentation, 63; miscellaneous, 20, 34; origin of name, 117, 130; pledged never to apply to the Stuarts, 58; reception of his Memorial by the Crown, 63; story in his Memorial, 53–61; unfounded tales, 16; varying signatures, 44; in *X* vs. *Y*, 131–33
early years: affection for Baden, Munich, Rhine Valley, 17, 82; childish letters, 17; date of birth, 16, 56; education, 18; military career, 20, 21; silence as to foster parents, 128; sisters, 16, 37
famous people met. *See* Canaris, Constantine; Lamartine; Maeri, Theresa; Staël, Mme de
finances: aid from Castries, 121; aid from Coutts (?), 72; aid from father, 119; aid from wife, 79, 135; bankers, 27, 41, 43, 51, 120, 122, 135; debts to Julien, 121; debts to Sampigny, 35, 37, 84; income from Vienna, 52, 122; losses in Russia, 26, 27, 51; pleads poverty, 62, 66, 77, 119; summarized, 118–23
later years: in Baden, 120; concerned with the "Sobieski" Stuarts, 112; death, 115; lack of data after 1835, 109; last journey to Spain, 113–15; London address, 115; in Naples, 110; obituary, 116; will, 115
the Memorial: audience with Regent denied, 52; early form of, 48, 49; episode with the French police, 70–73; plans for the future, 19, 67, 68; plans for presenting, 52; searches for documents, 39, 41, 47; text, 53–61
middle years: accident at Dresden, 136; accident at Pompeii, 82; accident at Vesuvius, 135; his "aunt", 73, 81, 135; first marriage, 76, 121; gossip about him, 78; hates Abbeville, 135, 136; the Herculès affair, 84, 85; resides at Abbeville, Neuwied, etc., 79; on the "St. Vincent", 80, 88, 91, 120; second marriage, 78; trips from Germany to Naples, 81; voyage with Alewyn and Dirck, 75, 76
personality: air of distinction, 127; aloofness, 29, 36–37, 64, 95, 125, 128; as art critic, 113; "charm", 127; C. M. Allen's account of, 112; easily delighted, 106, 107; gifted as a liar, 129; hates small bureaucrats, 52; modesty, 124; physical appearance, 81; protection of Mrs. B—— in Munich, 128; quick anger, 83; quick observation, 106–7; sentimental aspects, 88–89, 126; taste in books, 125
in Russia: as chamberlain, 23; departure, 26–29; love affairs, 24; social life, 24, 25, 58–59
travels: across the Alps on foot, 46; Athens, 88, 92, 93; Berne, 46; Delos, 93; early residence in Edinburgh, 87; favorite cities, 87; Genoa, 73; interest in the Levant, 20, 75, 87, 88, 91; love of wandering, 49, 51, 52; Naples, 73; projects for returning to Russia, 67, 72; at a Russian-Turkish review, 99–102; saw (?) the Ganges and Mississippi, 52; site of Troy, 94; Smyrna, 75, 103–6; summarized, 87–108; trips to Italy with his "aunt", 75, 81, *et passim*; Venice, 45; volcanoes, 91
Rohan estate in Haiti, 30, 31
Rohan-Guéméné, Ferdinand, Prince and Archbishop of Cambrai (father of Roehenstart), 10–14, 39
Rohan-Guéméné, Louis-Armand, Admiral, 12

Rohan-Guéméné, Louis-René, Cardinal, 4
Rohan-Guéméné, Princess Charlotte de, 30
Rothschild, C. M., 122, 135
Rothschild, N. M., 123, 135
Rousseau, J. J., 46, 99
Royal Archives (Windsor), 71

Saalfeld, Battle of, 23, 137–44
Sage, Henry, 11, 13
St. Albans, eighth Duke of, 113
Saint-Simon, Louis de, 61
Sampigny, Comte Gabriel, 37–38, 78, 79, 80, 83, 120
Sardent, Mlle, 31 n.
Savente, Duke of, 51
Saxe-Coburg, Ernest, Duke of, 85
Saxe-Coburg family, 23, 137
Schrader, John, 70
Scottish Historical Society, 71 n.
Sidmouth, Henry, first Viscount, 66, 70, 74
Smith, Bouchier, 78, 80
Smith, Louisa Constance (Roehenstart's second wife). *See* Stuart, Louise Constance
Smith, Sir Sidney, 20
Smythe (or Smith), Walter, 79, 80
Sobieski, James, 10
Sobieski Stuarts, 109–12, 124
Sofniew (bankrupt), 27, 119
Soyecourt, Comte de, 84
Staël, Mme de, 47, 99
Starynkewitch, Chancellor, 69
Stoddart, Sir J., 77
Stolberg, Louise von (wife of Prince Charles): and Alfieri, 2, 55; death, 77; life in Florence, 41–42; marriage, 2–3, 55; pension, 2, 55; relations with Roehenstart, 40, 60, 77, 78
Stuart, Aglae, 4
Stuart, Sir Charles (ambassador), 70
Stuart, Charles Edward A. M. *See* Roehenstart
Stuart, Charlotte: alleged marriage to Roehenstart, 56; children, vi, 4; death, 57, 62; early visit to Rome, 2, 3; education, 1, 7, 53; financial motivations, 4, 8, 39; legitimated, 55; mistress to Ferdinand, 3; her *petit jardin*, 9; removes to Paris, 3; secretly corresponds with Cardinal York, 6; her story, 1–10; will, 15, 56
Stuart, James Moray, 78, 111
Stuart, Louisa Constance (Roehenstart's second wife): feels neglected, 135; letters to her, 134–36; lives in France, 82, 109; marriage, 78, 79; not called countess, 79
Stuart, Maria Antoinetta Sophia (Roehenstart's first wife), 76
Stuart, Marie (?), 4
Stuart, Zemire (?), 4
Stuart papers acquired, 65, 77

Tayler, Henrietta, v, vi, 19, 69, 71
Theiner, Auguste, 12
Turnbull, Forbes and Co., 27, 59, 119

Villette, Pierre M., Abbé de (vicar general of Cambrai), 9
Walkinshaw, Clementine, Countess of Albestroff: financial troubles, 15, 54, 58; grandchildren, 15, 112; leaves Paris, 9; letters to, v; mistress of Prince Charles Edward, 53; mother of Charlotte, 1; signs away her "marriage", 54; will and papers, 40, 41, 47
Wall, William, 47, 65
Waters, James, Abbé, 10, 77
Watson, Dr. Robert, 77
Watson, Mr. (secretary ?), 66
Webb, Sir G., 99
Weck, Counsellor of Fribourg, 40, 41, 47
Westmorland, Lady, 45
White, Elizabeth C., 115
Württemberg, Alexander, Duke of, 18, 126
Württemberg, Antoinette, Duchess of: fails to send Roehenstart funds, 51, 67, 69, 119; patronage of Roehenstart, 22, 23, 28

15